D1442349

WILLIAMS
SONOMA
CALIFORNIA

# THE COMPLETE
# JUNIOR
# CHEF
## COOKBOOK

PHOTOGRAPHY BY
ERIN SCOTT

weldon**owen**

# CONTENTS

Unicorn Marble Bundt Cake (page 96)

# INTRODUCTION

Learning how to cook can be a fun and rewarding experience—especially when it results in delicious foods to share with family and friends. Once you have mastered some basic techniques, prepared a few recipes, and worked with new ingredients, there's no limit to the number and kinds of dishes you can create. With these easy-to-follow recipes, handy tips, and simple techniques as your guide, you will soon be cooking up breakfast, soups, salads, sandwiches, snacks, main dishes, and loads of tasty desserts.

When it comes to cooking, as with most skills that need to be learned, practice makes perfect! Every time you try a new recipe, you're almost sure to discover something new about a technique, ingredient, and/or your own personal taste and preferences. The recipes in this book include step-by-step instructions that guarantee you'll be able to make most of them with ease. You should always have an adult nearby when you are cooking, however, and ask for assistance when you need it. Grown-ups are great for helping sort out recipe directions and for keeping you safe when oven and stovetop heat or sharp knives or other tricky tools are involved.

Whether you want to make breakfast treats for a sleepover, a yummy snack for friends after school, or a special family meal, you'll find the dish you're looking for in this book. With these recipes in hand, you can cook up both old favorites—pizza, tacos, cupcakes—and new discoveries—summer rolls, frittata, madeleines—building your culinary confidence and impressing family and friends with your chef-pertise at the same time. So roll up your sleeves, tie on an apron, and get ready to begin an experience you will enjoy for a lifetime.

# BASIC TECHNIQUES

## ORGANIZATION

The first lesson every young chef needs to master is the practice of *mise en place*, literally "everything in its place." Before you begin to cook, read through the recipe from start to finish and get out the ingredients and equipment you'll need. Prepare the ingredients in advance as much as possible and assemble them neatly around your work area for easy access. The quickest way to ruin a recipe is to get halfway through it and realize you've forgotten to cut or measure an ingredient. And if your aim is to cook like a true chef, make sure to keep your hands and work area clean and put everything away as soon as you've finished using it. Also, be deliberate in everything you do, whether it's wielding a knife or tasting a salad dressing to see if it needs more salt. Your finished dishes will benefit from the extra effort.

## KNIFE SKILLS

Learning how to choose, hold, and use a knife is especially important for young cooks. When selecting a knife, consider the item to be cut, then pick out a knife that is both suitable for the task and feels comfortable in your hand.

### Holding a Knife

Hold the knife firmly by the handle, as if you were shaking someone's hand. Hold down the item you are cutting with your other hand, placing the flat side of the food down whenever you can. Curl under the fingers of the hand that's holding the food so your knuckles keep your fingertips out of harm's way. With the tip of the knife pointing down, start to cut, bringing the handle up and down and keeping the knife facing away from your body.

### Slicing

Place the food on the cutting board and steady it with your free hand, tucking your fingertips in toward your palm and keeping the side of the blade gently against your knuckles. With the knife held in your other hand, cut slices of the desired thickness.

### Chopping

Grasp the handle of a chef's knife and, with your other hand, steady the top of the knife blade near its tip against the cutting board. Raise and lower the knife handle in a chopping motion, slowly swinging the blade back and forth across the food until the desired texture is achieved.

### Dicing

Cut uniform slices, cut them again to make strips, then cut across the strips to make cubes.

## MEASURING

Use a set of measuring spoons (usually ¼ teaspoon, ½ teaspoon, 1 teaspoon, and 1 tablespoon) to measure small amounts of liquid and dry ingredients.

### Liquids

Measure liquid in clear measuring pitchers with rulers printed vertically on the side and a lip for pouring. Place the measuring pitcher on a flat surface, add the liquid, and check the measurement at eye level to make sure it is accurate.

### Dry Ingredients

Measure dry ingredients, such as sugar or flour, by spooning the ingredient into the proper-size flat-topped measuring cup, loosely heaping it, then level the ingredient by running the back of a knife flush over the rim of the cup.

## » HOW TO SLICE

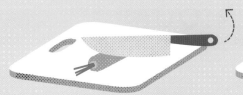

**1** Lay the item to be cut firmly on the cutting board, first trimming a thin slice from one side if needed to rest flat.

**2** Holding the item to be cut with curled fingers to keep fingertips safe, slice with the knife blade perpendicular to the cutting board.

**3** Slice the food while resting the flat side of the knife blade gently against your knuckles, allowing them to guide the width of your slices.

## » HOW TO CHOP

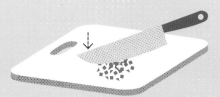
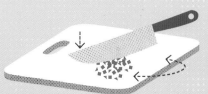

**1** Grasping the handle of the knife with one hand, hold the tip of the knife against the board with the other hand.

**2** Keeping the knife tip steady, raise the handle up and down in a chopping motion.

**3** As you move the handle up and down, sweep the knife back and forth in a slow arc until the ingredient is chopped as desired.

## » HOW TO DICE

**1** Cut the item to be diced in half. Lay each half, cut side down, on the cuttting board.

**2** Cut each half into even slices the same width as your intended dice, working lengthwise if the item is long.

**3** Cut the long slices into lengthwise strips, then turn and cut crosswise into dice.

## » HOW TO MEASURE

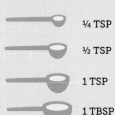

¼ TSP
½ TSP
1 TSP
1 TBSP

Check liquid measurements at eye level to ensure accuracy.

Spoon dry ingredients into a flat-topped measuring cup until mounded on top. Using the back of a knife, sweep off the excess level with the rim of the cup.

# BREAKFAST

# MAKE-YOUR-OWN GRANOLA

Homemade granola always tastes better than store-bought varieties, and you can add whatever you like to make it your own. Start with this great recipe, then swap in your own favorite nuts, seeds, and dried fruits—walnuts or almonds, sunflower or sesame seeds, blueberries or cherries—in place of what's here.

**1 PREHEAT THE OVEN**

Preheat the oven to 350°F. Line a rimmed baking sheet with parchment paper.

**2 MIX THE GRANOLA**

In a large bowl, combine the oats, pecans, coconut, pepitas, sugar, salt, and cinnamon and stir to mix well. In a small bowl, whisk together the oil and vanilla. In another small bowl, beat the egg white with a fork until frothy. Pour the oil mixture over the oat mixture and stir to coat evenly. Then pour the egg white over the oat mixture and stir gently until evenly mixed.

**3 BAKE THE GRANOLA**

Pour the mixture onto the prepared baking sheet, spreading it evenly. Bake the granola, carefully removing the pan from the oven to stir once or twice during baking, until the mixture is nicely toasted, about 35 minutes. Remove from the oven and let cool. Stir in the dried fruit just before serving or storing. Store in an airtight container at room temperature for up to 1 month.

2½ cups old-fashioned rolled oats

1 cup chopped pecans

½ cup unsweetened flaked dried coconut

½ cup pepitas (pumpkin seeds)

⅓ cup firmly packed brown sugar

¾ teaspoon salt

¾ teaspoon ground cinnamon

½ cup coconut oil or canola oil

1 teaspoon pure vanilla extract

1 large egg white

½ cup dried cranberries or golden raisins

**» FRESH GRANOLA** offers crunch and flavor to a bowl of creamy plain yogurt. Add fresh fruit and a drizzle of honey for a wholesome and delicious breakfast bowl.

# EASY FRENCH CREPES

In France, street vendors and restaurants alike sell these thin, delicate pancakes that they fold around both savory and sweet fillings. For lunch, swap out these sweet suggestions (and omit the sugar) for ham and a good melting cheese.

**1 MELT THE BUTTER**

Put the 2 tablespoons butter in a small microwave-safe bowl or cup. Microwave on high power until melted, about 20 seconds. Let cool.

**2 MAKE THE BATTER**

Pour the milk into a blender. Crack the eggs into the blender, then pour in the melted butter. Add the flour, granulated sugar, baking powder, and salt. Blend on low speed just to mix. Using a rubber spatula, scrape down the sides of the blender. Blend on high speed until smooth.

**3 COOK THE CREPES**

Place a 10-inch crepe pan or nonstick frying pan over medium-high heat. When the pan is hot, add about 1 teaspoon butter and spread it evenly over the bottom of the pan with a silicone spatula. Pour in about ⅓ cup of the batter all at once. Immediately tilt and swirl the pan so the batter evenly covers the bottom. Cook the crepe until lightly browned on the bottom (lift an edge with the spatula to see), about 2 minutes. Using the spatula, slide it under the center of the crepe and carefully flip it. When the second side is lightly browned, after about 2 minutes, carefully slide the crepe onto a serving plate. Serve the crepe at once, or repeat with the remaining crepe batter and filling, adding more butter to the pan as needed and stacking the crepes on the plate. Cover and keep warm until all are cooked.

**4 SERVE THE CREPES**

To serve, spread your choice of filling evenly over a crepe, then fold it first in half, and then into quarters. Sprinkle with powdered sugar and serve warm.

2 tablespoons unsalted butter, plus more for cooking the crepes

2 cups whole milk

2 large eggs

1½ cups all-purpose flour

1 tablespoon granulated sugar

½ teaspoon baking powder

½ teaspoon salt

Nutella, jam, or fresh strawberries and whipped cream for filling

Powdered sugar for dusting

# RASPBERRY-ALMOND SCONES

Small, crumbly, and only slightly sweet, scones can do double duty on the breakfast table and as an afternoon snack. For an easy variation, try blueberries instead of raspberries and chopped pecans rather than almonds.

**1 MAKE THE DOUGH**

Preheat the oven to 400°F. Line a baking sheet with parchment paper. In a bowl, mix the flour, 3 tablespoons of the sugar, the baking powder, and the salt. Scatter the butter over the top. Using a pastry blender or 2 knives, cut in the butter until the mixture resembles coarse crumbs. Stir in ½ cup of the almonds. Pour in the cream and stir just until combined. Using one hand, knead the dough against the side of the bowl just until it holds together.

**2 ROLL OUT & CUT THE SCONES**

Turn the dough out onto a lightly floured surface. Using a rolling pin, gently roll the dough into a rectangle about ½ inch thick. Cut the dough in half crosswise. Arrange the raspberries in a single layer over half of the dough. Place the other half of the dough on top. Using the rolling pin, roll out the dough again into a 9-inch round. Cut the dough through the center like the spokes of a wheel into 8 triangles. Transfer the scones to the prepared baking sheet.

**3 TOP THE SCONES**

In a small bowl, combine the egg white and the remaining 2 tablespoons sugar and stir briskly with a fork until frothy. Using a pastry brush, brush a little of the egg white mixture over the top of each scone. Transfer 2 teaspoons of the egg white mixture to a small bowl, add the remaining 2 tablespoons almonds, and toss to mix. Scatter the coated almonds over the the scones.

**4 BAKE THE SCONES**

Bake the scones until golden brown, 17–20 minutes. Let cool briefly on a wire rack, then serve warm or at room temperature.

2 cups all-purpose flour

5 tablespoons sugar

2½ teaspoons baking powder

¼ teaspoon salt

½ cup cold unsalted butter, cut into 1-inch chunks

½ cup plus 2 tablespoons slivered almonds

1 cup heavy cream

½ cup raspberries

1 large egg white

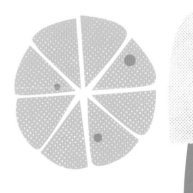

# PUFF PASTRY APRICOT TWISTS

Puff pastry is magical. It is made up of many, many paper-thin layers of butter trapped between many, many paper-thin sheets of dough. When it goes into a hot oven, all the layers puff up to create an airy, flaky pastry. Puff pastry dough is hard to make, but it is easy to find at a grocery store.

**1 THAW THE PASTRY**

Preheat the oven to 400°F. Line a baking sheet with parchment paper. Remove the puff pastry from the freezer and let thaw at room temperature for about 20 minutes.

**2 BRUSH THE PASTRY WITH JAM**

Place the pastry on a lightly floured work surface, unfold, and press flat. Using a pizza cutter or sharp knife, cut the sheet in half to make 2 rectangles. Using a pastry brush, evenly brush 1 rectangle with the jam. Place the uncovered rectangle on top. Put the egg white in a small bowl and beat lightly with a fork. Using the pastry brush, lightly brush the top of the pastry with some of the egg white. Sprinkle half of the sugar evenly over the top, pressing it in gently so it adheres. Turn the pastry over, brush the top side with the egg white, sprinkle with the remaining sugar, and again press to adhere.

**3 MAKE THE TWISTS**

Using the pizza cutter or knife, cut the pastry rectangle lengthwise into 6 equal strips. Twist the ends of each strip in opposite directions to give the strip a spiraled look, then transfer the twists to the prepared baking sheet, spacing them about 1½ inches apart. Refrigerate for 20 minutes.

**4 BAKE THE TWISTS**

Bake the pastry twists until they are golden and the jam is bubbling, about 15 minutes. Turn off the oven and leave the twists in the oven for 5 minutes longer to crisp. Carefully transfer the twists to a wire rack and let cool briefly, then serve warm.

1 sheet frozen puff pastry, about ½ lb

¼ cup apricot jam

1 large egg white

1 tablespoon turbinado sugar

# SCRAMBLED EGGS WITH CHEDDAR, SAUSAGE & ONIONS

Kielbasa sausage is originally from Poland. It is sold in most supermarkets and is usually made from pork, seasoned with garlic, and lightly smoked, though turkey kielbasa is also available. Can't find kielbasa? Linguica, a Portuguese smoked pork sausage, will work too.

**1 WHISK THE EGGS**

Crack the eggs into a large bowl. Add the milk and whisk just until blended. Season with salt and pepper.

**2 BROWN THE SAUSAGE**

In a large nonstick frying pan over medium-high heat, warm the oil. Add the green onions and sausage and cook, stirring frequently, until the onions are softened and the sausage is browned, about 5 minutes.

**3 SCRAMBLE THE EGGS**

Reduce the heat to medium-low, add the butter to the pan, and tilt and swirl the pan to coat the bottom evenly with the butter. Pour in the eggs and cook, without stirring, for 1 minute. Using a silicone spatula, gently stir the eggs, allowing the uncooked egg to run underneath the cooked egg. Cook until the eggs are mostly set, about 3 minutes, then stir in the cheese. Continue to stir the eggs gently until set, about 1 minute longer.

**4 SERVE THE EGGS**

Remove the pan from the heat, divide the eggs among 4 plates, and serve.

8 large eggs

2 tablespoons whole milk

Salt and freshly ground pepper

2 tablespoons olive oil

2 green onions, white and pale green parts, thinly sliced

6 oz kielbasa sausage, halved lengthwise and thinly sliced crosswise

1 tablespoon unsalted butter

¼ cup shredded Cheddar cheese

# ZUCCHINI, GREEN ONION & FONTINA FRITTATA

A frittata is an Italian omelet but, unlike its French cousin, which is rolled around its filling, the filling is mixed with the eggs and the frittata is served flat. When shredding the zucchini, be sure to keep your fingers safely away from the sharp holes of the grater-shredder.

**1 SHRED THE ZUCCHINI**
Using the large holes of a box grater-shredder, shred the zucchini onto paper towels. Spread out the shreds and sprinkle with a little salt. Let stand for about 20 minutes. Using paper towels, blot the zucchini as dry as possible. Meanwhile, preheat the oven to 375°F.

**2 WHISK THE EGGS**
Crack the eggs into a large bowl. Add the cream and basil and whisk just until blended. Stir in the cheese. Season with salt and pepper.

**3 COOK THE FRITTATA**
In an 8-inch nonstick ovenproof frying pan over medium-low heat, melt the butter. Add the onions and cook, stirring, until softened, about 2 minutes. Stir in the zucchini. Pour in the eggs and cook, without stirring, until the edges are set. Using a silicone spatula, lift the cooked edges to allow the raw egg to run underneath until no more runny egg is visible, 3–4 minutes. Place the pan in the oven and bake until the eggs are puffy and set, 8–10 minutes.

**4 SERVE THE FRITTATA**
Remove the frying pan from the oven and let the frittata cool for a few minutes. Asking an adult for help and using oven mitts, hold a serving plate upside down over the pan and turn the pan and plate together, releasing the frittata onto the plate. Cut into squares or wedges and serve warm or at room temperature.

2 small zucchini, about 7 oz total, trimmed

Salt and freshly ground pepper

8 large eggs

2 tablespoons heavy cream

1 tablespoon finely chopped fresh basil

¾ cup shredded fontina cheese

1 tablespoon unsalted butter

2 green onions, white part only, thinly sliced

# CHEESY BAKED EGGS WITH BACON

This dish is about as easy as it gets in the kitchen, plus everybody likes it. You just crack the eggs directly into the little baking dishes and they cook between layers of cheese. You can choose a different cheese, too. Just make sure it is a good melting cheese, like Monterey jack or Swiss.

## 1 COOK THE BACON
Preheat the oven to 300°F. Butter four 3½-inch ramekins. In a frying pan over medium-high heat, cook the bacon, stirring often, until crisp, about 5 minutes. Using a slotted spoon, transfer the bacon to paper towels to drain.

## 2 DICE THE TOMATO
Cut the tomato in half crosswise (through the "equator"). Squeeze out the seeds, using your finger to scoop out any seeds that remain. Now dice each half into ½-inch pieces.

## 3 LAYER THE INGREDIENTS
Divide half of the cheese evenly among the prepared ramekins, spreading it over the bottom of each dish. Crack an egg into each ramekin. Divide the remaining cheese evenly among the ramekins, sprinkling it over the eggs. Top with the bacon, tomato, chives, and bread crumbs, dividing each ingredient evenly. Sprinkle each ramekin with a little salt and pepper. Arrange the ramekins on a baking sheet (for easy transport to the oven).

## 4 BAKE THE EGGS & SERVE
Bake until the eggs are cooked, about 15 minutes. The eggs are ready when the whites are set but the yolks are still runny. If the crumbs have not lightly browned, turn the oven to the broiler setting and broil for 1–2 minutes. Serve hot.

Butter for greasing

2 bacon slices, diced

1 tomato

½ lb Gruyère cheese, coarsely shredded

4 large eggs

1 teaspoon chopped fresh chives, or 1 tablespoon thinly sliced green onion tops

¼ cup fresh bread crumbs

Salt and freshly ground pepper

**» SERVING TIP**
Spinach would be a great addition to this egg bake. Thaw 6 oz frozen spinach and squeeze dry. Divide it evenly among the ramekins, top with the cheese and other ingredients, and bake as directed.

# MEXICAN OMELET

With a little practice and a high-quality nonstick frying pan, making omelets can become an easy morning ritual. Once you learn the basic technique, try your own favorite ingredients for the filling. Start with a good melting cheese and stop there, or layer on vegetables, sliced meats, or crumbled bacon.

**1 PREPARE THE FILLING**

Assemble all of the ingredients for the omelet filling. Set aside.

**2 BEAT THE EGGS**

In a bowl, whisk together the eggs, cream, ¼ tsp salt, and a few grinds of pepper just until blended.

**3 MAKE THE OMELETS**

In a small frying pan, preferably nonstick, melt 1 teaspoon of the butter over medium heat, tilting the pan to cover the bottom evenly with butter. Pour half of the egg mixture into the pan and cook until the eggs have barely begun to set around the edges, about 30 seconds. Using a heatproof spatula, lift the cooked edges and gently push them toward the center, tilting the pan to allow the liquid egg on top to flow underneath, then cook for 30 seconds longer. Repeat this process, moving around the perimeter of the pan, until no liquid egg remains.

**4 FILL THE OMELETS**

When the eggs are almost completely set but still slightly moist on top, sprinkle half of the cheeses over half of the omelet. Scatter half each of the avocado and salsa over the cheese. Using the spatula, fold the untopped half of the omelet over the filled half to create a half-moon shape. Let the omelet cook for 30 seconds longer, then slide it onto a serving plate. Keep warm. Repeat to make a second omelet in the same manner and serve.

FOR THE FILLING

¼ cup shredded Cheddar cheese

¼ cup shredded Monterey jack cheese

½ avocado, pitted, peeled, and sliced

¼ cup fresh salsa

FOR THE OMELETS

4 large eggs

2 tablespoons heavy cream

Salt and freshly ground pepper

2 teaspoons unsalted butter

# HOW TO MAKE A PERFECT OMELET

**1**

Beat the eggs in a bowl.

**2**

Pour the eggs into the frying pan.

**3**

Tilt the pan (lifting the edge of the cooked egg with a heatproof spatula) to allow the uncooked eggs to run underneath.

**4**

Place the filling over half of the omelet.

**5**

Fold the uncovered half over the filling with the spatula.

**6**

Slide the omelet onto a plate (using the spatula as a guide).

# SWEET APPLESAUCE BREAD

If you buy the applesauce, check the jar carefully to make sure it is unsweetened or your bread will be too sweet. If you want some crunch, fold ¾ cup chopped walnuts into the batter just before scraping it into the loaf pan.

**1 MAKE THE BATTER**

Preheat the oven to 350°F. Grease an 8½ by 4½ by 2½-inch loaf pan. In a large bowl, combine the applesauce, sugar, oil, and vanilla and stir to mix well. In a small bowl, whisk the eggs until well blended. Stir the eggs into the applesauce mixture until evenly combined. In a second small bowl, combine the flour, baking soda, baking powder, cinnamon, allspice, nutmeg, and salt. Stir to mix well. Stir the flour mixture into the applesauce mixture just until evenly blended.

**2 BAKE THE BREAD**

Scrape the batter into the prepared bread pan. Bake the bread until a toothpick inserted into the center comes out clean, 55–60 minutes. Let cool in the pan on a wire rack for 10 minutes, then turn the bread out of the pan onto the rack. Turn the bread upright and let cool before serving.

½ cup canola oil, plus more for greasing the pan

1¼ cups unsweetened applesauce

¾ cup sugar

½ teaspoon pure vanilla extract

2 large eggs

1¾ cups all-purpose flour

1 teaspoon baking soda

½ teaspoon baking power

½ teaspoon ground cinnamon

½ teaspoon ground allspice

½ teaspoon ground nutmeg

¼ teaspoon salt

# BLUEBERRY STREUSEL MUFFINS

Buttermilk gives these muffins a delicious tangy flavor. In the old days when butter was made at home, buttermilk was the liquid that remained in the churn after the finished butter was scooped out. Then, as now, it was a baking staple.

**1 MAKE THE STREUSEL**

In a small bowl, combine the flour, sugar, and butter. Mix with your fingertips just until combined. Mix in the almonds. Set aside.

**2 PREPARE THE PAN**

Preheat the oven to 400°F. Butter and flour 12 standard muffin cups or line them with paper liners. (Alternatively, butter the 6 wide wells in a standard muffin top pan.)

**3 MELT THE BUTTER**

Put the 5 tablespoons butter in a small microwave-safe bowl and microwave on high power until melted, about 30 seconds. Let cool.

**4 MAKE THE BATTER**

In a bowl, mix the flour, sugar, baking powder, baking soda, and salt. In another bowl, whisk together the buttermilk, eggs, cooled butter, vanilla, and almond extract (if using). Pour the buttermilk mixture over the flour mixture and stir just until combined. Using a rubber spatula, fold in the blueberries. Divide the batter evenly among the prepared muffin cups, filling the standard muffin cups about three-fourths full and the muffin top cups completely full. Sprinkle the streusel evenly over the top.

**5 BAKE THE MUFFINS**

Bake the muffins until golden brown and a toothpick inserted into the center of a muffin comes out almost clean (just a few crumbs should cling to the toothpick), 20–25 minutes. Transfer the pan to a wire rack and let the muffins cool in the pan for 15 minutes, then turn them out onto the rack. Serve warm or at room temperature.

FOR THE STREUSEL

¼ cup all-purpose flour

2 tablespoons sugar

2 tablespoons unsalted butter, at room temperature

⅓ cup sliced almonds

FOR THE MUFFINS

5 tablespoons unsalted butter, plus more for greasing pan

2 cups all-purpose flour

⅔ cup sugar

½ teaspoon baking powder

½ teaspoon baking soda

¼ teaspoon salt

1 cup low-fat buttermilk

2 large eggs

½ teaspoon pure vanilla extract

¼ teaspoon pure almond extract (optional)

1½ cups fresh or frozen blueberries

# GOOEY CINNAMON ROLLS WITH VANILLA-ORANGE ICING

These huge cinnamon rolls are irresistible. Plus, you can make the dough and shape the rolls the night before you serve them, so all you need to do in the morning is put them in the oven. A lush vanilla icing offers the finishing touch, adding just the right note of sweet gooeyness to the just-baked rolls.

## 1 MAKE THE DOUGH

In a stand mixer fitted with the paddle attachment, combine the milk, granulated sugar, melted butter, eggs, and yeast. Add 4½ cups of the flour and the salt and beat on medium-low speed until a soft dough forms that does not stick to the bowl. If the dough is too wet, add a little more flour, 1 tablespoon at a time, as needed. Replace the paddle attachment with the dough hook and knead the dough on medium-low speed, again adding a little more flour if needed, until the dough is smooth but still soft, 6–7 minutes.

## 2 LET THE DOUGH RISE

Remove the bowl from the mixer stand. Shape the dough into a ball. Butter a large bowl. Add the dough ball to the bowl and turn the ball to coat it with the butter. Cover the bowl tightly with plastic wrap and place it in a warm spot. Let the dough rise until doubled in size, 1½–2 hours.

## 3 MAKE THE FILLING

Wash the mixer bowl and paddle attachment and return them to the mixer. Add the brown sugar, butter, and cinnamon to the bowl and beat on medium speed until combined, about 30 seconds.

FOR THE DOUGH

1 cup whole milk

½ cup granulated sugar

5 tablespoons unsalted butter, melted and cooled, plus more for greasing the bowl

3 large eggs

1 package (2¼ teaspoons) quick-rise yeast

4½–5 cups all-purpose flour, plus more for dusting

1¼ teaspoons salt

FOR THE FILLING

½ cup firmly packed light brown sugar

6 tablespoons unsalted butter, at room temperature

2 teaspoons ground cinnamon

*Continued on page 28 »*

» Continued from page 27

## 4 SHAPE THE ROLLS

Lightly flour a work surface. Turn out the risen dough onto the floured surface. Press down on the dough to release any air bubbles. Dust the top with flour. Using a rolling pin, roll out the dough into a rectangle about 14 by 16 inches, with a long side facing you. Spread the filling evenly over the dough, leaving a 1-inch border uncovered along the top and bottom edge. Starting at the long side farthest from you, roll up the rectangle toward you into a log. Pinch the seam to seal. Cut the log crosswise into 8 equal slices. Each slice should be about 2 inches thick.

## 5 LET THE ROLLS RISE

Butter a 9 x 13-inch baking pan or a large, heavy ovenproof frying pan. Arrange the slices, with a cut side up, in the prepared pan. Cover the pan loosely with plastic wrap and let the rolls rise in a warm spot until doubled in size, 1¼–1½ hours. (Alternatively, refrigerate the rolls overnight until doubled in size, 8–12 hours, then let stand at room temperature for 1 hour before baking.)

## 6 BAKE THE ROLLS

Preheat the oven to 350°F. Remove the plastic wrap and bake the rolls until they are golden brown, about 30 minutes. Let cool in the pan on a wire rack for 15 minutes.

## 7 MAKE THE ICING

While the rolls are cooling, make the icing: Sift the confectioners' sugar into the clean bowl of the stand mixer and add the cream cheese, butter, vanilla, and orange zest. Beat on low speed (preferably using the paddle attachment) until crumbly. Gradually beat in enough of the milk to make a thick but pourable icing. Drizzle the icing over the warm rolls, or pour the icing over the rolls and spread evenly over the top. Let cool for at least 15 minutes longer. Serve the rolls warm or at room temperature.

FOR THE VANILLA-ORANGE ICING

1½ cups powdered sugar

2 oz cream cheese, at room temperature

2 tablespoons unsalted butter, at room temperature

½ teaspoon pure vanilla extract

Grated zest of 1 orange

About ¼ cup whole milk

**» GO FRUITY-NUTTY**
These jumbo cinnamon rolls are pretty darn great on their own but, in the spirit of believing there's always room for improvement, consider scattering 1 cup finely chopped pecans or raisins over the filling before rolling up the dough.

# HOW TO MAKE CINNAMON ROLLS

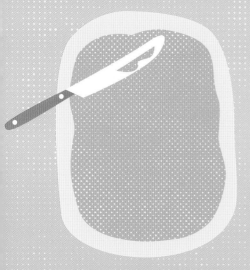

**1**

Spread the filling evenly over
the dough rectangle, leaving a
1-inch edge.

**2**

Beginning at a long side,
roll the dough up into a log,
enclosing the filling inside.

**3**

Cut the log crosswise into
8 slices, each one about
2 inches thick.

**4**

Place the rolls cut side up into a
9 x 13-inch baking pan, spacing
them evenly.

**5**

Cover loosely with plastic
wrap and let the rolls rise
until doubled in size.

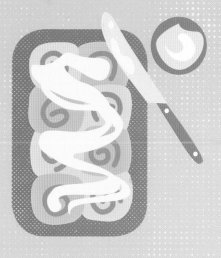

**6**

Drizzle the icing over the
warm rolls and spread evenly
over the top.

# MILE-HIGH DUTCH BABY

Despite the name, this recipe is all-American—a combination pancake and popover invented at a restaurant in Seattle, Washington. It puffs up dramatically in the oven, creating a perfect bowl for summertime's sweet, juicy peaches.

**1 MELT THE BUTTER FOR THE BATTER**

Place a 12-inch ovenproof frying pan in the oven and preheat the oven to 425°F. Put the butter in a small microwave-safe bowl and microwave on high power until melted, about 20 seconds. Let cool.

**2 MAKE THE BATTER**

In a blender, combine the milk, flour, salt, and eggs and blend until smooth. With the motor running, drizzle in 1 tablespoon of the melted butter and blend until incorporated.

**3 BAKE THE PANCAKE**

Carefully remove the frying pan from the hot oven. Pour the remaining 1 tablespoon melted butter into the pan and, using a pastry brush, brush the butter over the pan bottom and sides. Pour in the batter and immediately return the pan to the oven. Bake until puffed and golden, 15–20 minutes.

**4 PREPARE THE PEACHES**

While the pancake bakes, cut the peaches in half and remove the pits, then cut in slices. Put the peach slices in a bowl and add the granulated sugar and lemon juice. Toss to mix. Set aside.

**5 SERVE THE PANCAKE**

When the pancake is ready, carefully remove the pan from the oven and pour the peaches into the pancake's bowl-like center. Sprinkle the peaches with the almonds. Using a fine-mesh sieve, dust the pancake lightly with powdered sugar. Cut into wedges and serve with whipped cream, if desired.

FOR THE BATTER

2 tablespoons unsalted butter

⅔ cup whole milk

⅔ cup all-purpose flour

¼ teaspoon salt

3 large eggs

FOR THE PEACHES

3 ripe peaches or nectarines

2 tablespoons granulated sugar

1 teaspoon fresh lemon juice

¼ cup lightly toasted sliced almonds

Powdered sugar for dusting

Whipped cream for serving (optional)

# BUTTERMILK PANCAKES

Thomas Jefferson, the third president of the United States, is said to have been a big fan of pancakes. Following his years in office, he reportedly returned to his home in Monticello with a pancake recipe from a French chef in Washington, D.C.

**1 MELT THE BUTTER**

Put the 3 tablespoons butter in a small microwave-safe bowl or cup and microwave on high power until melted, about 25 seconds. Let cool.

**2 MAKE THE BATTER**

In a large bowl, stir together the flour, baking powder, baking soda, and salt. In a medium bowl, whisk together the eggs, buttermilk, and melted butter. Add the egg mixture to the flour mixture and stir until incorporated. (The batter will still be slightly lumpy.)

**3 COOK THE PANCAKES**

Place a stove-top griddle or large frying pan over medium heat. When the griddle is hot, add about 1 tablespoon butter and spread it evenly over the surface of the griddle with a spatula. Pour about ⅓ cup batter onto the griddle for each pancake, spacing them about 2 inches apart. Cook until the edges are golden and bubbles form on the surface, about 2 minutes. Using the spatula, flip the pancakes and continue cooking until golden brown on the bottom and cooked through, about 1 minute longer. Using the spatula, transfer the pancakes to a large plate and keep warm. Repeat with the remaining batter, adding more butter to the griddle as needed.

**4 SERVE THE PANCAKES**

Serve the pancakes warm with maple syrup or one or more of the suggested toppings.

3 tablespoons unsalted butter, plus more for cooking the pancakes

1½ cups all-purpose flour

1½ teaspoons baking powder

¾ teaspoon baking soda

¼ teaspoon salt

2 large eggs

2 cups low-fat buttermilk

Maple syrup, warmed, for serving (optional)

**PANCAKE TOPPINGS**

Try any of these combos:

- Fresh blueberries, whipped cream, and blueberry syrup

- Diced fresh pineapple, macadamia nuts, shredded dried coconut, and maple syrup

- Peanut or almond butter, crumbled crisply cooked bacon, and maple syrup

- Fresh strawberries, whipped cream, and strawberry syrup

- Finely chopped apples with cinnamon-sugar, maple syrup

# CRISPY WAFFLES WITH MIXED BERRIES

Dutch "wafles" came to America with the pilgrims in the 1600s. These early settlers sometimes hosted "wafle frolics," parties in which the crisp cakes were served sweet with maple syrup and molasses, or savory with meat stew.

**1 MELT THE BUTTER**

Preheat a waffle maker according to the manufacturer's directions. Put the butter in a small microwave-safe bowl or cup and microwave on high power until melted, about 30 seconds. Let cool.

**2 MAKE THE BATTER**

In a large bowl, stir together the flour, sugar, baking powder, and salt. In a medium bowl, whisk together the eggs, milk, melted butter, and vanilla. Add the egg mixture to the flour mixture and stir until no lumps remain.

**3 COOK THE WAFFLES**

Coat the inside of the waffle maker with nonstick cooking spray. Ladle ½ to ¾ cup batter onto the center of the lower grid; it should spread to within about ½ inch of the edge. Close the lid and cook until the steam subsides or a light on the waffle maker indicates the waffle is ready, 2-4 minutes. The waffle should be golden brown and cooked through. Carefully open the waffle iron, transfer the waffle to a plate, and keep warm. Repeat with the remaining batter, spraying the waffle iron with more cooking spray if needed to prevent sticking.

**4 SERVE THE WAFFLES**

Put the berries in a serving bowl. Serve the waffles warm. Pass the berries and maple syrup at the table for everyone to add as desired.

4 tablespoons unsalted butter

1½ cups all-purpose flour

3 tablespoons sugar

1 tablespoon baking powder

¼ teaspoon salt

2 large eggs

1½ cups whole milk

1 teaspoon pure vanilla extract

Nonstick cooking spray for the waffle iron

2 cups mixed berries, such as whole raspberries, blueberries, and blackberries and sliced strawberries

Maple syrup, warmed, for serving

# NUTELLA-FILLED DOUGHNUTS

Nutella creates an exceptionally oozy and delicious surprise inside each of these sugar-coated doughnuts. Don't worry if the dough seems sticky. A soft dough guarantees a tender doughnut. When it is time to start frying, be sure to have a grown-up alongside you at the stove.

## 1 WARM THE MILK & BUTTER

In a small saucepan over medium heat, combine the milk and butter and heat, stirring, until the butter is melted and the mixture is hot but not boiling. Test the temperature with an instant-read thermometer; it should be about 125°F. Remove from the heat.

## 2 MAKE THE DOUGH

In a stand mixer fitted with the paddle attachment, combine 2½ cups of the flour, the sugar, salt, and yeast and beat on low speed briefly to mix. Add the hot milk mixture, raise the speed to medium, and beat until well blended. Add the eggs and vanilla and continue to beat on medium speed until fully incorporated, about 2 minutes. Add the remaining ¾ cup flour and beat until the dough is well blended and smooth, about 1 minute longer. The dough will not pull away from the sides of the bowl and will still be somewhat sticky.

## 3 LET THE DOUGH RISE

Scrape the dough into a large bowl, cover with a clean kitchen towel, and place the bowl in a warm spot. Let the dough rise until well risen and increased in bulk (it may almost double in size), about 45 minutes. Meanwhile, line a baking sheet with waxed paper and brush the paper with oil. Line a second baking sheet with paper towels and place it near the stove.

¾ cup whole milk

3 tablespoons unsalted butter

3¼ cups all-purpose flour

⅓ cup granulated sugar

½ teaspoon salt

1 package (2½ teaspoons) quick-rise yeast

2 large eggs

½ teaspoon pure vanilla extract

Canola or peanut oil for brushing and deep-frying

½ cup superfine sugar

⅔ cup Nutella

## 4 CUT OUT THE DOUGHNUTS

Generously flour a work surface. Turn the dough out onto the floured surface. Using a floured rolling pin, roll out the dough into a round about 10 inches in diameter and ½ inch thick. Using a 3-inch round pastry cutter, cut out as many rounds as possible. Using a wide metal spatula, carefully transfer the rounds to the oiled waxed paper. Gather up the scraps and repeat rolling and cutting out rounds, flouring the work surface and rolling pin again as needed to prevent sticking. Cover the cutouts with a clean kitchen towel and let rise in a warm spot for 30 minutes. They should look soft and puffy but will not double in size.

## 5 FRY THE DOUGHNUTS

Pour oil to a depth of 2 inches into a deep, heavy sauté pan and heat over medium heat to 360°F on a deep-frying thermometer (or if you have a deep fryer, use it). Using a slotted spoon, carefully lower 2–5 doughnuts into the hot oil and deep-fry until they are dark golden on the underside, about 1½ minutes. Using the slotted spoon, carefully turn them over and cook until they are dark golden on the second side, about 1 minute longer. Using the slotted spoon, transfer them to the towel-lined baking sheet. Repeat to fry the remaining doughnuts, allowing the oil to return to 360°F between batches.

## 6 COAT & FILL THE DOUGHNUTS

Spread the sugar on a large plate or in a wide, shallow bowl. Fit a pastry bag with a ¼-inch round tip and spoon the Nutella into the bag. When the doughnuts are just cool enough to handle, working quickly, roll them in the sugar to coat on all sides. Using the tip of a small, sharp knife, cut a ½-inch-long slit in the side of each doughnut. Press the tip of the pastry bag gently into each slit and pipe about 2 teaspoons of the Nutella into the doughnut. Arrange the donuts on a platter and serve warm.

**》 WATCH THE OIL TEMPERATURE**

When doughnuts are fried at the proper temperature, they absorb little oil. If the frying temperature is too low, oil seeps into the dough, creating soggy doughnuts. If the oil is too hot, the outside of the doughnuts will be overcooked. The moment you add anything to hot oil, the temperature of the oil drops, so be sure to let the oil return to the original temperature before adding each new batch of dough.

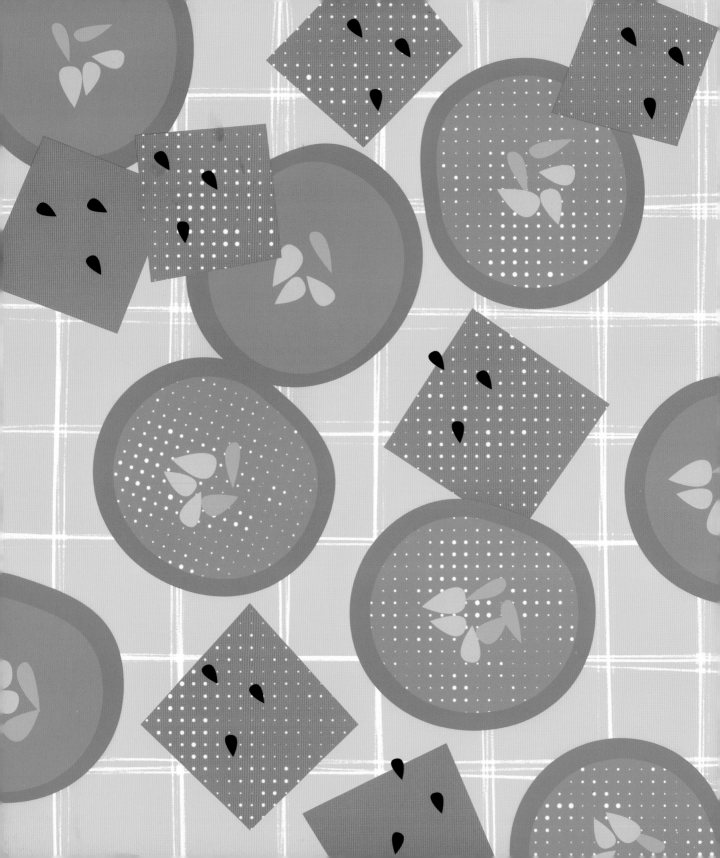

# SOUPS, SALADS & SANDWICHES

# WONTON SOUP

Making wontons at home is a fun cooking activity. Be sure to seal the edges of the wonton wrappers securely, or the filling will tumble out in the boiling water.

**1 MAKE THE WONTON FILLING**
In a food processor, combine the pork and ginger. Process until smooth. Add the water chestnuts, green onion, cilantro, soy sauce, and egg. Season with salt and pepper. Process again until smooth.

**2 MAKE THE WONTONS**
Fill a small bowl with water and set it on the work surface. Working with 1 wonton wrapper at a time, place it on the work surface and moisten 2 edges with cold water. Place 2-3 teaspoons of the filling in the center and fold the wrapper in half, forming a triangle. Press the edges firmly to seal. Bring the two bottom corners of the triangle to meet across the top of the mound and pinch together to seal. If they do not stick, moisten with a little water. Repeat until all the wonton wrappers and filling are used up.

**3 MAKE THE SOUP**
Discard the mushroom stems. Slice the mushroom caps. In a saucepan, bring the broth to a boil over medium heat. Add the bok choy, carrot, and sliced mushrooms. Simmer for 2 minutes.

**4 COOK THE WONTONS**
Meanwhile, bring a large saucepan three-fourths full of water to a boil over high heat. Add the wontons, reduce the heat to medium, and simmer gently until the wontons float to the surface and the skins are tender, about 3 minutes. Using a wire skimmer, carefully lift out the wontons and divide evenly among 4-6 bowls.

**5 SERVE THE SOUP**
Ladle the soup over the wontons, garnish with the green onion tops, and serve.

FOR THE WONTONS

¼ lb diced pork, chicken, or shrimp

1½ teaspoons peeled and grated fresh ginger

2 tablespoons chopped water chestnuts

1½ tablespoons chopped green onion, white part only

1 tablespoon chopped fresh cilantro

1 tablespoon light soy sauce

1 egg

Salt and ground white pepper

24 square wonton wrappers

2-3 dried shiitake mushrooms, soaked in hot water to cover for 30 minutes and drained

6 cups chicken broth

¾ cup packed small bok choy leaves

½ carrot, peeled and sliced

1 green onion, pale green part only, thinly sliced

» FRESH WONTONS
can be made up to 2 days
ahead of serving. Place
them in a single layer
on a baking sheet, cover
with plastic wrap, and
store in the refrigerator.

# CREAMY TOMATO SOUP

A bowl of tomato soup and a tasty sandwich are a classic lunch combo. Try the Chicken Salad Sliders (page 44) or BLAST Club Sandos (page 43) alongside. Top each steaming bowl with crunchy croutons or your own favorite garnish.

**1 MAKE THE SOUP**

In a large saucepan over medium heat, warm the oil and butter. Add the onion and cook, stirring often, until softened and translucent, 5–7 minutes. Add the garlic and cook, stirring frequently, for 2 minutes longer. Add the tomatoes and their juices and the broth, raise the heat to high, and bring to a boil. Reduce the heat to medium-low and simmer, stirring occasionally, for 20 minutes.

**2 PURÉE THE SOUP**

Remove the saucepan from the heat. You can purée the soup using an immersion blender or a stand blender. To use an immersion blender, let the tomato mixture cool slightly, submerge the end of the blender stick in the soup, and carefully blend, moving the stick around the pan, until smooth. To use a stand blender, let the soup cool to lukewarm. Then, working in batches, transfer the soup to the blender and blend until smooth. Pour each batch into a large bowl until all the soup is puréed, then return all the soup to the saucepan.

**3 FINISH & SERVE THE SOUP**

Return the saucepan to medium-low heat and stir in the cream. Season with ½ teaspoon each salt and pepper, stir well, then taste and add more salt and pepper if needed. Heat, stirring, until a steady stream of steam rises from the surface. Ladle the soup into individual bowls and serve.

1 tablespoon olive oil

2 tablespoons unsalted butter

1 yellow onion, coarsely chopped

2 cloves garlic, minced

1 can (28 oz) diced tomatoes with juices

4 cups chicken or vegetable broth

½ cup heavy cream

Salt and freshly ground pepper

# CHICKEN PHO

This version of the iconic Vietnamese soup calls for some signature ingredients of Southeast Asian cooking, such as rice noodles, bean sprouts, fish sauce, and toasted whole spices. It's an excellent choice when you have leftover cooked chicken on hand.

**1 SOAK THE RICE NOODLES**

In a bowl, combine the noodles with boiling water to cover and let soak for 10 minutes. Drain and set aside.

**2 TOAST THE SPICES**

In a small frying pan over medium heat, combine the star anise, coriander seeds, cinnamon, and cloves. Toast the spices, stirring frequently, until fragrant, 2–3 minutes. Remove from the heat.

**3 MAKE THE SOUP BROTH**

In a saucepan over medium-high heat, combine the broth, ginger, fish sauce, sugar, and toasted spices and bring to a boil. Reduce the heat to low and simmer for 30 minutes until fragrant. Remove from heat and pour through a fine-mesh sieve into a heatproof container. (The pot will be heavy, so ask for help.) Return the strained broth to the pan and return to a boil over medium-high heat. Add the noodles and cook for 5 minutes. Remove from the heat.

**4 SERVE THE SOUP**

While the broth returns to a boil, arrange the lime wedges, cilantro leaves, and bean sprouts in separate piles on a plate and set it on the table. If you like spicy food, put the chile and hot sauce on the table, too. Using tongs, transfer the noodles to 2 large soup bowls, dividing them evenly, then top with the chicken, dividing it evenly. Ladle the hot broth into the bowls and serve. Add the lime juice, cilantro, bean sprouts, and hot sauce and chile as you like.

3 oz rice noodles

1 star anise pod

1 tablespoon coriander seeds

1 cinnamon stick

2 whole cloves

4 cups chicken broth

2-inch piece fresh ginger, peeled and minced

1 tablespoon Asian fish sauce

1 teaspoon sugar

½ lime, cut into 4 wedges

2 tablespoons fresh cilantro or basil leaves

1 cup mung bean sprouts

1 small red chile, seeded and thinly sliced, for serving (optional)

Hot-pepper sauce, such as Sriracha, for serving (optional)

1 cup shredded Cooked Chicken (page 122)

» CLASSIC CLUB sandwiches like this one are always served as "double-deckers." If it seems like too much of a mouthful, just skip the middle slice of bread.

# BLAST CLUB SANDOS

It's easy to remember the five essential ingredients in this new and improved club sandwich: B=bacon, L=lettuce, A=avocado, S=sprouts, and T=tomatoes. Add them all up between three pieces of mayo-topped bread for a top-rate lunch.

**1 COOK THE BACON**

Fry the bacon in a small frying pan over medium heat, turning once, until crisp, 3–4 minutes. Transfer the bacon to a paper towel–lined plate to cool, then cut in half.

**2 MAKE THE SANDWICHES**

To make the first sandwich, spread ½ tablespoon of the mayonnaise over 1 toasted bread slice. Using a spoon, carefully scoop the avocado half from its skin and place, cut side down, onto a cutting board. Cut the avocado half lengthwise into thin slices. Arrange half of the avocado slices on the bread over the mayonnaise. Scatter half of the sprouts over the avocado, then arrange 2 turkey slices on top. Spread ½ tablespoon of the mayonnaise over another toasted bread slice, then place the slice, mayonnaise side down, on the turkey. Spread the top side of the bread with ½ tablespoon mayonnaise. Top with a lettuce leaf and half the tomato slices. Break the bacon strips in half and arrange 3 bacon slice halves in a single layer over the tomatoes. Spread a third toasted bread slice with ½ tablespoon mayonnaise. Place it, mayonnaise side down, on top of the bacon, pressing down gently. Repeat with the remaining ingredients to make the second sandwich.

**3 SERVE THE SANDWICHES**

Holding the sandwich firmly on a cutting board, use a serrated bread knife to cut the sandwiches in half on the diagonal. Transfer to 2 plates and serve.

3 slices bacon

4 tablespoons mayonnaise

6 slices sandwich bread, toasted

½ avocado, pit removed

½ cup sprouts, such as alfalfa or sunflower

4 slices cooked turkey, about ¼ lb total

2 large iceberg lettuce leaves

½ large red tomato, thinly sliced

# CHICKEN SALAD SLIDERS

The sweet, mellow, and licorice-like flavor of tarragon is a natural partner for chicken and a nice addition to chicken salad. Serve it in soft slider buns (as here), or spoon the salad onto crisp lettuce leaves for an easy roll-up. To save time, use purchased rotisserie chicken in place of home-cooked chicken.

**1 MAKE THE CHICKEN SALAD**

In a bowl, whisk together the sour cream, mustard, 3 tablespoons mayonnaise, tarragon, and honey. Using a rubber spatula, fold in the chicken, celery, green onions, and parsley. Season with a little bit of salt and lots of pepper.

**2 ASSEMBLE & SERVE THE SLIDERS**

Cut the slider buns in half horizontally and arrange, cut side up, on a work surface. Spread a little mayonnaise over the cut sides of both halves. Place a lettuce leaf on each bun bottom. Divide the chicken salad evenly among the lettuce-topped bottoms. Close with the bun tops, cut side down, and serve.

3 tablespoons sour cream

1 tablespoon Dijon mustard

3 tablespoons mayonnaise, plus more for spreading

1 tablespoon chopped fresh tarragon

1 teaspoon honey

2 cups diced Cooked Chicken (page 122)

2 celery stalks, finely diced

2 green onions, white part only, thinly sliced

2 tablespoons chopped fresh flat-leaf parsley

Salt and freshly ground pepper

8 slider buns, such as sweet Hawaiian buns, sourdough rolls, or dinner rolls

8 small lettuce leaves, such as bibb or baby romaine

# GREEK GYROS WRAPS

These easy wraps are a delicious riff on the traditional Greek gyro of marinated meat slices—lamb, pork, or chicken—tightly layered on a vertical spit, cooked, "shaved" off in thin strips, then wrapped in flatbread for a hearty sandwich. Here, marinated chicken thighs stand in for the shaved meat.

**1 MARINATE THE CHICKEN**

In a small bowl or cup, combine the lemon juice, vinegar, oregano, oil, garlic, salt, and a generous grind or two of pepper. Stir until blended. Put the chicken in a large, heavy-duty lock-top plastic bag. Pour in the marinade, seal closed, and squish to coat the meat evenly with the marinade. Place in the refrigerator and marinate for at least 2 hours or up to 1 day.

**2 COOK THE CHICKEN**

Position a rack in the upper third of the oven and preheat to 450°F. Remove the chicken from the marinade and discard the marinade. Arrange the chicken thighs, smooth side down, on a wire rack over a rimmed baking sheet. Bake, turning once after 10 minutes, until cooked through, 25–30 minutes. Transfer to a plate and let cool for 5 minutes.

**3 HEAT THE BREADS**

Meanwhile, reduce the oven temperature to 400°F. Wrap the breads in aluminum foil. Place in the oven to warm for 5 minutes.

**4 ASSEMBLE THE WRAPS**

Place four 10-inch squares of aluminum foil on a work surface. Unwrap the breads and place each bread on a foil square. Spread each bread with about ¼ cup of the tzatziki. Sprinkle the tomatoes and red onion over the tzatziki, dividing each of them evenly. Cut the chicken into bite-size pieces and divide among the breads. Fold up each wrap, using the foil to secure the bottom two-thirds of the wrap and leaving the top exposed. Serve warm with extra tzatziki.

FOR THE MARINADE

1 tablespoon fresh lemon juice

2 teaspoons white wine vinegar

1 tablespoon dried oregano

1 tablespoon olive oil

2 cloves garlic, minced

½ teaspoon salt

Freshly ground pepper

1 lb boneless, skinless chicken thighs

4 flatbreads, such as Greek pita or Indian naan or chapati

1 cup Tzatziki (page 122), plus more for serving

1 cup cherry tomatoes, halved

¼ small red onion, finely diced

# TACO SALAD

Whip up some of this easy salsa dressing for an authentic taco salad or swap it out for your own favorite. Purchased taco seasoning adds quick flavor to the meat. Check the grocery-store aisle stocked with Mexican foods, or the aisle with gravy and sauce mixes, and select any brand that looks good to you.

**1 MAKE THE VINAIGRETTE**

In a small jar or other small container with a tight-fitting cover, combine the salsa, vinegar, lime juice, and a dash each of salt and pepper. Add 4 tablespoons of the oil, cover, and shake until well mixed. Taste the dressing and add more oil and/or salt and pepper if needed.

**2 COOK THE BEEF**

Place a large frying pan over medium heat. Add the ground beef and cook, using a wooden spoon to break it up into small pieces, until cooked through, 8–10 minutes. (If it looks too greasy, ask an adult to help you pour off any fat from the pan.) Add the seasoning mix and water to the pan, raise the heat to high, and bring to a boil. Reduce the heat to low and simmer, stirring often, until the liquid is absorbed, about 12 minutes.

**3 BEGIN ASSEMBLING THE SALAD**

While the meat is cooking, cut off the stem of the lettuce half and cut the lettuce into thin slices. Separate the slices into long shreds. Divide the lettuce evenly among the tortilla bowls or regular salad bowls. Top each bowl with equal amounts of the tomatoes, beans, and avocado.

**4 FINISH THE SALAD & SERVE**

When the meat is done, use a slotted spoon to divide it evenly among the salads. Sprinkle the cheese on top, dividing it evenly. Spoon an equal amount of the dressing over each salad, then serve, topped with tortilla chips, if desired.

FOR THE SALSA VINAIGRETTE

1 tablespoon store-bought mild tomato salsa

1 tablespoon red wine vinegar

2 teaspoons fresh lime juice

Salt and freshly ground pepper

4–6 tablespoons extra-virgin olive oil

FOR THE SALAD

1 lb ground beef

¼ cup taco seasoning mix (about ½ package)

⅔ cup water

½ head iceberg lettuce

4 Tortilla Bowls (page 124) or tortilla chips for serving (optional)

3 plum tomatoes, diced

1 cup drained canned black or pinto beans, rinsed

1 avocado, halved, pitted, peeled, and cut into ¾-inch cubes (see page 65)

1½ cups shredded Cheddar cheese

**›› TORTILLA BOWLS** make tasty vessels for serving this chunky salad. Or, scoop the salad into regular bowls and crumble tortilla chips on top.

# THE WEDGE SALAD WITH HOMEMADE RANCH DRESSING

Yes, ranch dressing gets its name from a real ranch! It was invented by Steve Henson, who, along with his wife, Gayle, ran the Hidden Valley Ranch, a dude ranch near Santa Barbara, California. Today, it is the most popular salad dressing in the United States, with Italian dressing number two in demand.

**1 MAKE THE DRESSING**

In a bowl, combine the mayonnaise, buttermilk, parsley, shallot, and garlic and stir until well mixed. Stir in ½ teaspoon salt and ¼ teaspoon pepper, then taste and add more salt and pepper if needed.

**2 CUT THE LETTUCE INTO WEDGES**

Ask an adult to help you cut the lettuce head, as it can be hard to keep it from rolling. Using a large, sharp knife, cut off the stem end of the iceberg head. Next, cut the lettuce head in half through the stem end. Then, cut each half in half again to make 4 large wedges.

**3 ASSEMBLE THE SALAD**

Place each wedge, cut side up, on a salad plate. Spoon an equal amount of the dressing over each wedge. Scatter any combination of the cherry tomatoes, blue cheese crumbles, and/or bacon crumbles over the top, if using. Sprinkle each wedge with parsley and serve.

**FOR THE DRESSING**

½ cup mayonnaise

½ cup low-fat buttermilk

1 tablespoon minced fresh flat-leaf parsley, or 1 teaspoon dried parsley

1 teaspoon minced shallot, or ½ teaspoon onion powder

1 clove garlic, minced, or ½ teaspoon garlic powder

Salt and freshly ground pepper

1 head iceberg lettuce

1 cup cherry tomatoes (optional)

¼ cup blue cheese crumbles (optional)

¼ cup crumbled fried bacon (optional)

Finely chopped fresh flat-leaf parsley for garnish

# WATERMELON, NECTARINE & CUCUMBER SALAD

Watermelon is more than 90% water, which is why everyone likes to eat a big slice on a hot day. It has a crisp and mellow flavor that pairs well with both sweet and savory ingredients. Watermelons can be tricky to cut, so you might want some help with that step.

**1 CUT THE WATERMELON**

Make sure you have some help with this step, as it is hard to cut a big, round watermelon. On a cutting board, using a long, sharp knife, cut the watermelon in half through the stem end. Place the halves cut side down and cut in half again, then cut each half crosswise into thin slices. Using a small, sharp knife, cut along the rind to remove it from each slice, then cut the watermelon into bite-size cubes.

**2 CUT THE NECTARINES & CUCUMBERS**

Find the natural indent in a nectarine and, using the small knife, start at the stem end and cut all the way around the nectarine. Twist the halves in opposite directions to separate them. Lift out and discard the pit. Place the halves, cut side down, on a cutting board and cut lengthwise into thin slices. Repeat with the remaining nectarine. Cut both ends off each cucumber, then thinly slice the cucumbers crosswise.

**3 MAKE THE SALAD**

In a large, shallow serving bowl, gently toss together the watermelon, nectarine, and cucumber slices. Drizzle the oil and vinegar over the mixture, sprinkle with feta and mint, and serve.

1 mini seedless watermelon, about 4 lb

2 nectarines

2 Persian cucumbers

2 tablespoons extra-virgin olive oil

2 tablespoons white balsamic vinegar

3 oz feta cheese, crumbled

½ cup fresh mint leaves

# MAINS

# PARMESAN SPAGHETTI SQUASH WITH TURKEY MEATBALLS

From the outside, the canary yellow spaghetti squash offers no hint as to how it got its name. But once it's cooked, the inside transforms into spaghetti-like strands.

**1** **COOK THE SQUASH**
Make the squash as directed.

**2** **MAKE THE MEATBALLS**
While the squash is baking, line a rimmed baking sheet with parchment paper. In a large bowl, combine all the meatball ingredients. Mix with a spoon or clean hands until evenly blended. To shape each meatball, scoop out a tablespoon-size portion of the turkey mixture, roll it between your palms to form a ball, and place on the prepared baking sheet. Repeat with the remaining turkey mixture, setting the balls well apart in a single layer on the pan.

**3** **BAKE THE MEATBALLS**
When the squash is done, remove it from the oven, and raise the oven temperature to 450°F. When the oven is ready, bake the meatballs until browned and cooked through, about 15 minutes.

**4** **PREPARE THE SQUASH**
Scrape the squash into strands and prepare as directed (page 123).

**5** **COMBINE THE SAUCE & MEATBALLS**
Warm the sauce in a large saucepan over low heat, stirring occasionally. When the meatballs are done, transfer them to the sauce. Heat, stirring often and gently, for about 5 minutes.

**6** **SERVE THE SPAGHETTI & MEATBALLS**
Divide the squash evenly among 4 plates. Ladle the sauce and meatballs over the top. Sprinkle with Parmesan and serve hot.

1 roasted Parmesan Spaghetti Squash (page 123)

FOR THE MEATBALLS
1 lb ground dark-meat turkey

½ cup dried bread crumbs

⅓ cup freshly grated Parmesan cheese

¼ yellow onion, finely chopped

1 large egg

1 tablespoon milk

1 tablespoon finely chopped fresh flat-leaf parsley

1 tablespoon fresh oregano, or 1½ teaspoons dried oregano

Salt and freshly ground pepper

2⅓ cups Marinara Sauce, homemade (page 124) or store-bought

Freshly grated Parmesan cheese, for serving

# POTATO CHIP CHICKEN TENDERS

For dinner in a hurry, bake up a batch of these crisp, potato chip–encrusted bites. They are best served hot from the oven with your favorite dip alongside. For an easy gluten-free version, simply skip the flour-dipping step.

**1 PREPARE THE BAKING SHEET**
Preheat the oven to 375°F. Line a baking sheet with aluminum foil. Place a baking rack on the baking sheet and coat with cooking spray.

**2 CRUSH THE POTATO CHIPS**
Put the potato chips in a large, lock-top plastic bag, press out the air, and seal the bag closed. Run a rolling pin over the bag until the chips are crushed to the size of coarse bread crumbs.

**3 COAT THE CHICKEN**
Pour the crushed chips into a shallow bowl. (You should have about 3 cups.) Crack the eggs into another shallow bowl and beat until blended. Put the flour into a third shallow bowl. Season the chicken pieces with salt and pepper. Working with 1 or 2 chicken pieces at a time, dip first in the flour, turning to coat both sides and shaking off the excess, then dip into the egg, turning to coat and allowing the excess to drip back into the bowl, then place in the crushed potato chips, turning to coat both sides and pressing the crumbs gently onto the chicken. As you work, place each coated piece on the prepared baking rack.

**4 BAKE & SERVE THE CHICKEN**
Bake the chicken until golden brown and the chicken is cooked throughout, 15-20 minutes. Serve hot, with the dip on the side.

Nonstick cooking spray

1 bag (8 oz) potato chips

2 large eggs

½ cup all-purpose flour

1 lb small boneless, skinless chicken breasts, cut lengthwise into thick slices

Salt and freshly ground pepper

Ranch dressing (page 48), barbecue sauce, or ketchup for dipping

# STEAMED SALMON WITH ASPARAGUS & BELL PEPPER

One of the best things about this recipe—in addition to it tasting so good!—is that you don't have lots of dirty pots and pans to wash. The fish and vegetables cook together in individual foil packets, making cleanup a breeze.

**1** **MAKE THE SAUCE**

Preheat the oven to 450°F. Cut 4 sheets of aluminum foil each about 18 inches long. In a blender, combine the lime juice, soy sauce, sugar, sesame oil, ginger, garlic, and red pepper flakes and blend until smooth.

**2** **ASSEMBLE THE FISH PACKETS**

Place 1 foil sheet on a work surface. Place a salmon steak or fillet on one half of the foil. Mound one-fourth each of the asparagus and bell pepper on top of the salmon and top with one-fourth of the green onions. Drizzle with about 2 tablespoons of lime-soy mixture. Fold the uncovered half of the foil over the salmon and crimp the edges together on three sides to seal securely. Place the packet on a large rimmed baking sheet. Repeat with the remaining ingredients to assemble 3 more packets, adding them to the baking sheet.

**3** **BAKE & SERVE THE FISH**

Bake the salmon for 10 minutes. Remove from the oven and let cool slightly. Carefully open the packets to release the trapped steam. Transfer the salmon and vegetables to 4 individual plates and serve.

2 tablespoons fresh lime juice

1 tablespoon plus 1 teaspoon low-sodium soy sauce

1 tablespoon firmly packed golden brown sugar

1 tablespoon Asian sesame oil

1-inch piece fresh ginger, peeled and roughly chopped

1 clove garlic

Pinch of red pepper flakes

4 salmon steaks or fillets, about 6 oz each

¼ lb asparagus, tough ends removed, spears cut on the diagonal into 2-inch pieces

1 red bell pepper, halved, seeded and thinly sliced

6 green onions, thinly sliced

# THAI CHICKEN LETTUCE CUPS

Serve these healthy lettuce wraps with peanut sauce, or mix your favorite vinaigrette with chopped cilantro and mint for a sauce with zesty flavor. Cook the chicken on a grill or grill pan, or swap it out for purchased rotisserie chicken.

**1 MARINATE THE CHICKEN**

In a small bowl, mix the oil, mint, cumin, cayenne pepper, salt, and black pepper. Put the chicken in a large, heavy-duty lock-top plastic bag. Add the marinade, seal closed, and squish to coat the chicken. Let marinate in the refrigerator for 30 minutes.

**2 HEAT THE GRILL OR GRILL PAN**

With an adult to help you if needed, prepare a charcoal or gas grill for direct grilling over medium-high heat. Brush and oil the grill grate. (Or, lightly oil a grill pan and place over medium-high heat.)

**3 GRILL THE CHICKEN**

Remove the meat from the marinade and pat dry with paper towels; discard the marinade. Place the chicken on the grill or grill pan. Cook, turning once, until lightly browned and cooked throughout, 4–6 minutes on each side. Transfer the chicken to a cutting board and let cool. Using a sharp knife, cut the meat on the diagonal into slices and transfer to a small serving bowl; set aside.

**4 PREPARE THE REMAINING INGREDIENTS**

Bring a small pan of water to a boil over high heat. Add the noodles, remove from the heat, and let stand until soft, about 10 minutes. Put the carrots, cucumber, bean sprouts, peanuts, cilantro, and sauce in separate bowls. Drain the rice noodles and place in a bowl.

**5 SERVE THE LETTUCE CUPS**

Set all the vegetables, the nuts, sauce, and lettuce leaves on the table. For each lettuce cup, invite diners to fill a lettuce leaf with chicken, rice noodles, carrots, cucumber, bean sprouts, peanuts, and cilantro as desired, then drizzle some of the sauce over the top.

FOR THE CHICKEN

¼ cup olive oil

2 tablespoons finely chopped fresh mint

1 tablespoon ground cumin

¼ teaspoon cayenne pepper

¼ teaspoon *each* salt and freshly ground black pepper

1 lb boneless, skinless chicken breasts

2 oz dried rice stick noodles

2 carrots, peeled and julienned or shredded

½ English cucumber, thinly sliced

2 cups mung bean sprouts

¼ cup chopped roasted peanuts

¼ cup fresh cilantro leaves

⅓ cup Peanut Sauce, homemade (page 122) or store-bought

8 whole red leaf, butter, or iceberg lettuce leaves

# SLOPPY JOES

Who invented the Sloppy Joe? Some say it was a cook named José in Havana, Cuba. Others say it is named for a bar in Key West, Florida. And still others claim a cook at a diner in Sioux City, Iowa, created it in the 1930s. Why "sloppy"? It could refer to either the inventor or the sandwich!

**1 COOK THE MEAT FOR THE FILLING**

Place a large frying pan over medium-high heat. If you are using turkey, add the oil to the pan to keep it from sticking. Add the meat and cook, using a wooden spoon to break it up into small pieces, until evenly cooked, 8–10 minutes. Ask an adult to help you pour off the fat from the pan. Reduce the heat to medium-low and add the brown sugar, onion, paprika, chili powder, and garlic powder. Cook, stirring, until blended, about 2 minutes.

**2 FINISH THE FILLING**

Add the tomato sauce, tomato paste, Worcestershire sauce, and vinegar to the meat mixture. Stir until well mixed. Raise the heat to high and bring to a boil. Immediately reduce the heat to medium-low and cook, stirring often to blend the flavors, about 5 minutes longer. Season with salt and pepper.

**3 ASSEMBLE & SERVE THE SANDWICHES**

Place a bun bottom, cut side up, on each of 4 plates. Spoon an equal amount of the meat mixture over each bun bottom. Close with the bun tops. Serve hot.

1 tablespoon olive oil, if using turkey

1¼ lb ground beef or turkey

2 tablespoons firmly packed golden brown sugar

2 tablespoons dried minced onion

1 teaspoon paprika

1 teaspoon chili powder

½ teaspoon garlic powder

1 can (15 fl oz) tomato sauce

2 tablespoons tomato paste

2 tablespoons Worcestershire sauce

2 teaspoons red wine vinegar

Salt and freshly ground pepper

4 hamburger buns, split

# CHILI WITH CHEESE

Chili powder is not just one thing. It is a mix of seasonings, with cayenne pepper delivering the heat, and usually cumin, garlic powder, oregano, and paprika rounding out the flavor. If you want to up the heat in this dish, add a little more chili powder to the pot.

**1** **BROWN THE BEEF**

In a large, heavy pot over medium heat, warm the oil. Add the onion and cook, stirring often, until soft and translucent, about 5 minutes. Add the beef and garlic and cook, using a wooden spoon to break the meat up into small pieces, until the beef is browned, 5-7 minutes.

**2** **ADD THE SEASONINGS & TOMATOES**

Add the chili powder, cumin, basil, and oregano and stir to mix well. Stir in the broth, crushed tomatoes and their juices, and tomato paste. Reduce the heat to medium-low and simmer, stirring occasionally, until the mixture has a thick, chunky consistency, about 1 hour.

**3** **ADD THE BEANS & SERVE**

Add the beans and simmer, stirring occasionally, until heated through and the flavors are blended, about 5 minutes longer. Season with salt and pepper. Ladle the chili into 4-6 bowls and sprinkle the cheese evenly over each bowl. Serve hot.

1 tablespoon olive oil

¾ cup chopped yellow onion

1½ lb ground beef

4 cloves garlic, minced

2 tablespoons plus 2 teaspoons chili powder

1½ teaspoons ground cumin

½ teaspoon dried basil

½ teaspoon dried oregano

2 cups chicken broth

1 can (14 oz) crushed tomatoes

¼ cup tomato paste

1 can (15½ oz) chili beans in sauce

Salt and freshly ground pepper

½ cup shredded Cheddar cheese

# COCONUT SHRIMP WITH SWEET ORANGE DIPPING SAUCE

Shredded coconut gives these tasty golden-crusted shrimp a mild sweetness. Deep-frying requires heating lots of oil to a high temperature, so always have an adult nearby (or go for the oven-baking option given at right).

**1 HEAT THE OIL**

Pour canola oil to a depth of 3–4 inches into a deep, heavy pot and heat over medium heat to 350°F on a deep-frying thermometer. Line 1 baking sheet with parchment paper. Line a second baking sheet with paper towels. Preheat the oven to 200°F.

**2 BREAD THE SHRIMP**

Spread the flour in a shallow bowl. Crack the eggs into another shallow bowl and beat until blended. In a third shallow bowl, mix the coconut and bread crumbs, then season with salt and pepper. Working with a few shrimp at a time, toss the shrimp in the flour, coating evenly and tapping off the excess. Next, dip the shrimp into the egg, allowing the excess to drip back into the bowl. Finally, toss the shrimp in the bread crumb mixture and place on the parchment-lined baking sheet until ready to fry.

**3 FRY THE SHRIMP**

When the oil is ready, using a wire skimmer or slotted spoon, lower 3 or 4 shrimp into the hot oil and fry until golden, about 3 minutes. Using the skimmer or slotted spoon, transfer the shrimp to the paper towel–lined baking sheet and place in the oven to keep warm until all are cooked. Repeat to fry the remaining shrimp.

**4 SERVE THE SHRIMP**

In a small bowl, stir together the marmalade and hot water. Serve the shrimp hot with the orange marmalade for dipping.

Canola oil for deep-frying

1½ cups all-purpose flour

3 large eggs

1½ cups sweetened shredded dried coconut

1½ cups bread crumbs

Salt and freshly ground pepper

1 lb jumbo peeled and deveined shrimp (21–25 size)

¼ cup orange marmalade

1 tablespoon hot water

>> BAKE THE SHRIMP
instead of frying them,
if you like. Place the shrimp
on a greased wire rack over
a baking sheet and bake
at 425°F for 10–15 minutes.

# ORECCHIETTE WITH SAUSAGE

Orecchiette means "little ears," which is exactly what these small, round pasta shapes look like. They make a great receptacle for trapping delicious bits of sausage and greens. If you cannot find them, farfalle, penne, or other short pastas will do.

**1 PREPARE THE BROCCOLI RABE & SAUSAGE**

Using a vegetable peeler, peel away the thick skin from the lower portion of each broccoli stalk. Cut the stalks into 1-inch lengths. Place in a bowl, add cold water to cover, and let stand for 1 hour. Bring a large pot of salted water to a boil over high heat. Add the broccoli rabe and cook for 1 minute, then transfer to a bowl and set aside. Using a measuring cup, scoop ½ cup of the cooking water from the pot and set aside. Reserve the remaining water in the pot.

**2 MAKE THE SAUCE & BREAD CRUMBS**

Place a frying pan over medium heat and add 2 tablespoons of the oil. Add the garlic and red pepper flakes and cook, stirring, for 1 minute. Add the sausage meat and cook, stirring to break up the sausage with a wooden spoon, until browned, 5–7 minutes. Add the broccoli rabe and cook, stirring, until heated through, about 2 minutes. Season with salt and pepper.

Meanwhile, make the bread crumbs: In a frying pan over medium-low heat, warm 1 tablespoon oil. Add the bread crumbs and cook, stirring, until golden, 2–3 minutes. Season to taste with salt and pepper. Set aside until ready to serve.

**3 PREPARE THE PASTA**

Return the water in the pot to a boil. Add the pasta and cook according to the package directions. Drain the pasta in a colander set in the sink. Add the pasta and remaining 4 tablespoons oil to the sauce in the pan and toss over medium heat to coat the pasta evenly with the sauce. Transfer to a serving bowl and sprinkle with the bread crumbs and Parmesan. Serve hot.

2 lb broccoli rabe, ends trimmed

7 tablespoons olive oil

4 cloves garlic, minced

Pinch of red pepper flakes

¾ lb sweet Italian sausage, casings removed

Salt and freshly ground pepper

¼ cup panko bread crumbs

1 lb orecchiette or other pasta of your choice

Freshly grated Parmesan cheese for serving

# TORTELLINI ALFREDO

More than a century ago, Alfredo Di Lelio, a Roman chef, gained fame for serving a simple but very rich dish of fettuccine with butter and cheese, proudly naming it after himself. Here, his idea is dressed up with tortellini and ham or peas.

**1 MAKE THE SAUCE**

In a saucepan over medium heat, combine the cream, ½ cup cheese, butter, a pinch each of salt and pepper, and the nutmeg (if using). Heat, stirring often with a wooden spoon, until the cheese and butter are melted. Reduce the heat to low and simmer, stirring occasionally, until thickened, about 15 minutes.

**2 COOK THE PASTA**

While the sauce is simmering, bring a large pot of water to a boil over high heat. Add 1 teaspoon salt and then the tortellini. Reduce the heat to medium-high and boil the tortellini gently until tender, 3–4 minutes or according to the package directions. Add the peas or ham (if using) during the last 1 minute of cooking. Drain the tortellini in a colander set in the sink.

**3 TOSS THE PASTA WITH THE SAUCE & SERVE**

Immediately transfer the tortellini to a serving bowl. Top the tortellini with the sauce and stir, turning the pasta gently to coat it evenly with the sauce. Sprinkle with more cheese and the parsley, if using. Serve hot.

¾ cup heavy cream

½ cup freshly grated Parmesan cheese, plus more for sprinkling

3 tablespoons unsalted butter

Salt and freshly ground pepper

Pinch of ground nutmeg (optional)

1 package (9 oz) store-bought refrigerated tortellini

1 cup fresh or frozen peas or diced ham (optional)

1 teaspoon minced fresh flat-leaf parsley (optional)

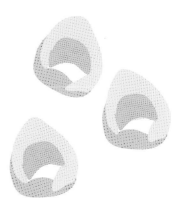

# TROPICAL BUDDHA BOWLS

What are Buddha bowls? They are all about being grateful for and mindful of what you are eating. By arranging the ingredients separately and beautifully, each unique flavor can be appreciated on its own with little embellishment.

**1 PREPARE THE QUINOA**
Prepare the quinoa as directed. Keep warm until ready to serve.

**2 MAKE THE VINAIGRETTE**
While the quinoa is cooking, make the vinaigrette. In a jar with a lid, combine the oil, lime juice, vinegar, water, and sugar. Place the lid on top, secure tightly, and shake well until evenly mixed. Season with salt and pepper and set aside.

**3 CUT THE MANGO & AVOCADO**
Hold the mango on a narrow side on a cutting board. Using a large, sharp knife, cut just to one side of the center to cut the mango flesh from the wide flat pit. Turn the mango and cut the flesh from the other side. Using a small, sharp knife, cut off the mango peel, dice or slice the flesh, and set aside. Using the small knife, cut into the center of the avocado, cutting all the way around the avocado when you reach the big round pit in the center. Separate the avocado halves. Use the tip of a spoon to remove the pit, then remove the peel, and dice or slice the avocado. Set aside.

**4 ASSEMBLE THE BOWLS**
Set all the toppings on the work surface. Divide the quinoa evenly among 4 bowls. Arrange the mango, avocado, chicken (if using), coconut, and cilantro in rows on top of each bowl, dividing each ingredient evenly. Place the kale in a bowl. Shake the vinaigrette again, then drizzle 1 tablespoon of the vinaigrette over the kale and toss to mix. Arrange the dressed kale in a row over the quinoa and sprinkle the macadamia nuts evenly over the top. Serve the bowls. Pass the remaining vinaigrette at the table.

Coconut-Ginger Quinoa
(page 123)

FOR THE VINAIGRETTE
¼ cup olive oil

1 tablespoon fresh lime juice

1 tablespoon white wine vinegar

1 tablespoon water

¼ teaspoon sugar

Salt and freshly ground pepper

FOR THE TOPPINGS
1 mango

1 avocado

1 cup diced Cooked Chicken
(page 122), optional

½ cup unsweetened shaved
dried coconut, toasted

¼ cup packed fresh
cilantro leaves

2 cups loosely packed baby kale
or mixed salad greens

½ cup chopped macadamia nuts

# GRILLED CHICKEN SATAY

Satay—meat, poultry, or seafood skewers cooked over a charcoal or wood fire—
is eaten all over Southeast Asia, sold by both street food vendors and restaurants.

**1 MARINATE THE CHICKEN**

In a bowl, combine the coconut milk, garlic, sugar, curry powder,
½ teaspoon each salt and pepper, and the lime juice. Whisk until
evenly blended. Set aside.

Cut the chicken breasts lengthwise into ¾-inch-wide strips. Using
a meat pounder, gently pound the chicken strips until they are about
¼ inch thick. Do not pound them too hard or they will tear. Add the
chicken to the coconut milk marinade and stir to coat well. Cover
with plastic wrap and refrigerate for at least 2 hours or up to 1 day.

**2 MAKE THE PEANUT SAUCE**

Make the peanut sauce as directed. Set aside until ready to serve.

**3 HEAT THE GRILL & ASSEMBLE THE SKEWERS**

Ask an adult to help you prepare a charcoal or gas grill for direct
grilling over medium-high heat. Brush the grill grate clean and then
oil the grate. (Alternatively, lightly oil a grill pan and place over
medium-high heat.) Soak 12–16 bamboo skewers in water to cover
for at least 15 minutes to prevent them from burning on the grill.

Remove the chicken from the marinade and pat dry with paper
towels; discard the marinade. Thread the chicken strips lengthwise
onto each soaked skewer, weaving the skewer through the chicken.

**4 GRILL & SERVE THE SATAY**

Place the skewers on the grill grate directly over the fire or on the
hot grill pan. Grill, turning once or twice, until golden brown and
cooked through, 6–8 minutes. Transfer to a large platter and serve
with the sauce for dipping.

½ cup full-fat coconut milk

1 clove garlic, minced

1½ teaspoons firmly packed
golden brown sugar

1 teaspoon curry powder

Salt and freshly ground pepper

Juice of ½ lime

1½ lb boneless, skinless
chicken breasts

Peanut Sauce (page 122)

# CHEESY SPINACH CALZONES

Calzones are the turnovers of the pizza world. Here, they hide a creamy, oozy mix of three different cheeses and good-for-you spinach inside a golden crust.

**1 MAKE THE FILLING**

In a large frying pan over medium heat, warm the 2 tablespoons oil. Add the onion and cook, stirring often, until translucent, about 5 minutes. Stir in the garlic and cook, stirring, for 1 minute. Add the spinach, cover, and cook until tender, about 3 minutes. Drain the spinach mixture in a colander set in the sink and let cool. Press firmly on the spinach to remove as much excess liquid as possible. Transfer the mixture to a bowl. Add the ricotta, Parmesan, and mozzarella cheeses and mix well. Season with salt and pepper.

**2 SHAPE THE DOUGH**

Position racks in the center and lower third of the oven and preheat the oven to 400°F. Oil 2 large baking sheets. Divide the pizza dough into 6 equal portions. Shape each portion into a ball. Place the balls on a lightly floured work surface and cover with a kitchen towel.

**3 FILL THE CALZONES**

Using a rolling pin, roll out 1 ball of dough into a 7-inch round. Brush the dough edge lightly with water. Place one-sixth of the spinach-cheese mixture over half of the round, leaving a 1-inch border uncovered. Fold the dough over to enclose the filling. Using a fork, crimp the edges together to seal well. Pierce the top of the calzone with the fork to create a vent for steam to escape, and transfer to a prepared baking sheet. Repeat with the remaining dough and filling, putting 3 calzones on each baking sheet. Brush the calzones with oil.

**4 BAKE & SERVE THE CALZONES**

Place a pan on each oven rack and bake the calzones until golden, about 20 minutes. Carefully transfer the calzones to a wire rack and let cool for at least 10 minutes. Serve warm.

2 tablespoons olive oil, plus more as needed

1 yellow onion, finely chopped

2 cloves garlic, finely chopped

10 oz baby spinach

1 cup ricotta cheese

½ cup freshly grated Parmesan cheese

¼ lb fresh mozzarella cheese, finely diced

Salt and freshly ground pepper

2 balls Pizza Dough (page 124)

All-purpose flour for dusting

# PIZZA MARGHERITA

This popular pizza was invented in Naples, Italy, in the late nineteenth century to welcome Queen Margherita, the reigning monarch, who was visiting the city. The pizza maker chose the three toppings, basil, mozzarella, and tomatoes, in honor of the colors of the Italian flag, green, white, and red.

**1 READY THE PIZZA DOUGH**

Place the dough on a lightly floured surface. Press and stretch the dough into a round 12 inches in diameter. If the dough springs back as you shape it, let it rest for 5–10 minutes, then continue. Place a rack in the bottom third of the oven and preheat to 435°F.

**2 ADD THE TOPPINGS**

Line a baking sheet with parchment paper and sprinkle lightly with cornmeal. Place the dough circle on the prepared baking sheet. Brush the entire dough round with oil and season with salt and pepper. If using the sauce, spread it evenly over the dough with a spoon, leaving a 1-inch border uncovered on the edge. Sprinkle on the cheese, then top with the tomato slices. Season again with salt and pepper.

**3 BAKE THE PIZZA & SERVE**

Bake in the lower third of the oven until the crust is golden, 12–15 minutes. Remove the baking sheet from the oven, drizzle the pizza with a little oil, and let cool for a few minutes. Slide the pizza onto a cutting board. Scatter basil leaves over the pizza, cut into wedges, and serve hot.

1 ball Pizza Dough (page 124)

Cornmeal for dusting

Extra-virgin olive oil for brushing and drizzling

Salt and freshly ground pepper

1 cup Marinara Sauce (page 124) or store-bought pizza sauce (optional)

3 ripe plum tomatoes, thinly sliced

½ lb fresh mozzarella cheese, thinly sliced and then torn into 1-inch pieces

Fresh basil leaves for garnish

# CARNE ASADA SOFT TACOS WITH FRESH GUACAMOLE

In Mexico, carne asada (grilled beef) is sometimes served with side dishes—beans and rice and salad—but it is even better wrapped in tortillas for tacos or burritos. Make sure to slice the beef across the grain for the most tender meat.

**1 MARINATE THE MEAT**

In a large, heavy-duty lock-top plastic bag, combine the oil, onions, garlic, vinegar, chili powder, cumin, and pepper. Seal the bag closed and squish the bag to mix the ingredients well. Open the bag, add the meat, seal closed again, and squish to coat the meat evenly with the marinade. Let marinate for about 10 minutes.

**2 WARM THE TORTILLAS**

Preheat the oven to 400°F. Wrap the tortillas in aluminum foil and place in the oven until warm, about 5 minutes. Turn off the oven and leave the tortillas in the oven to stay warm until ready to use.

**3 GRILL THE STEAK**

Lightly oil a grill pan and place over medium-high heat. When the pan is hot, remove the meat from the marinade and pat dry with paper towels; discard the marinade. Place the steak on the grill pan and cook, turning once, until done to your liking, 3–4 minutes on each side for medium-rare. Transfer the steak to a cutting board, tent with aluminum foil, and let rest for 5 minutes.

**4 ASSEMBLE & SERVE THE TACOS**

Slice the steak across the grain into thin strips and mound on a plate. Add any juices that accumulated on the cutting board to the steak strips. Spoon the meat onto the warm tortillas, dividing it evenly. Top the meat with a spoonful of guacamole, fold the tortillas in half to make tacos, and serve. Pass the pico de gallo at the table.

¼ cup olive oil

4 green onions, white and pale green parts, thinly sliced

2 cloves garlic, minced

3 tablespoons red wine vinegar

½ teaspoon chili powder

1 teaspoon ground cumin

¼ teaspoon freshly ground pepper

1 lb skirt or flank steak

8 corn or flour tortillas, 8 inches in diameter

Guacamole for serving

Pico de gallo for serving

# SWEET POTATO TACOS WITH BLACK BEANS, CORN & AVOCADO

These all-veggie tacos are so tasty and colorful, no one realizes they are entirely meat-free and packed full of super-delicious superfoods. Add a little dollop of sour cream to each one for a rich finish, if you like.

**1 BAKE THE SWEET POTATO**

Preheat the oven to 425°F. Pile the sweet potato in the center of a rimmed baking sheet. Drizzle with 2 tablespoons of the oil and toss to coat evenly. Sprinkle with the chili powder and season with salt and pepper and toss again to coat evenly. Spread the sweet potato in a single layer. Bake, stirring once halfway through baking, until tender, about 15 minutes.

**2 WARM THE TORTILLAS**

Wrap the tortillas in aluminum foil and place in the oven about 5 minutes before the sweet potato is ready. After the sweet potato is removed, turn off the oven and leave the tortillas in the oven to stay warm until ready to use.

**3 PREPARE THE BEANS**

Just before the sweet potato is ready, in a frying pan over medium heat, warm the remaining 1 tablespoon oil. Add the onion and cook, stirring, until translucent, about 5 minutes. Add the garlic and cook, stirring often, for 1 minute longer. Stir in the cumin and coriander, then add the beans and stir until heated through, 1–2 minutes.

**4 ASSEMBLE & SERVE THE TACOS**

Unwrap the tortillas and place 2 tortillas on each of 4 plates. Top each tortilla with one-eighth each of the sweet potato, beans, corn, avocado, cheese, and cilantro and finish with a squeeze of lime juice. Fold the tortillas in half to make tacos and serve.

1 large sweet potato or yam, about 1¼ lb, peeled and cut into ½-inch dice

3 tablespoons olive oil

⅛ teaspoon chili powder

Salt and freshly ground pepper

8 corn tortillas, about 8 inches in diameter

½ small yellow onion, finely chopped

1 clove garlic, minced

½ teaspoon ground cumin

¼ teaspoon ground coriander

1 can (14½ oz) black beans, drained and rinsed

¾ cup frozen corn, thawed and drained

½ avocado, peeled and cut into 8 slices

½ cup crumbled feta cheese

½ cup fresh cilantro leaves

2 limes, halved

# FISH TACOS WITH MANGO SALSA

Mexico has about 6,600 miles of coastline, which means there's lots of fishing going on. Plus, it is the world's fifth largest producer of mangoes. Put the two together, and you have a natural south-of-the-border favorite.

**1 MAKE THE SALSA**

In a small bowl, combine the mango, chile, cilantro, and lime juice and stir to mix well. Season with salt and a generous amount of pepper. Cover and refrigerate until ready to serve.

**2 WARM THE TORTILLAS**

Preheat the oven to 400°F. Wrap the tortillas in aluminum foil and place in the oven to warm, about 5 minutes. Turn off the oven and leave the tortillas in the oven to stay warm until ready to use.

**3 PREPARE THE CABBAGE**

Using a sharp knife, cut the cabbage crosswise into thin slices, then separate the slices into shreds. Set aside.

**4 COOK THE FISH**

Lightly season the fish fillets on both sides with salt and pepper. Heat the oil in a large nonstick frying pan over medium-high heat. When the oil is hot, carefully slip the fish fillets into the pan and cook until browned on the bottom, about 3 minutes. Using a silicone spatula, carefully turn the fillets over and continue to cook until browned on the second side, 2–3 minutes longer.

**5 ASSEMBLE THE TACOS & SERVE**

Transfer the fish to a plate. Using 2 forks, break the fish into small chunks, discarding any bones. Unwrap the tortillas and place 2 tortillas on each of 4 plates. Fill each tortilla with one-eighth of the fish chunks, one-eighth of the cabbage, and about 2 tablespoons of the mango salsa. Top with the avocado slices and a squeeze of lemon juice, if using. Fold the tortillas in half to make tacos. Serve hot.

FOR THE MANGO SALSA

1 large just-ripe mango, peeled, pitted, and finely chopped (see page 65)

1 small fresh red chile, seeded and minced

2 tablespoons chopped fresh cilantro

2 tablespoons fresh lime juice

Salt and freshly ground pepper

8 corn tortillas, 8 inches in diameter

½ small head green cabbage

1 lb firm white fish fillets, such as mahimahi, halibut, or sea bass

1 tablespoon olive oil

1 avocado, halved, pitted, peeled, and sliced (see page 65), optional

1 lemon, halved (optional)

# FRESH SUMMER ROLLS WITH MANGO & AVOCADO

Once you master the technique for these easy rice paper rolls, you'll likely discover your own favorite combination of filling ingredients.

**1  PREPARE THE FILLINGS**

Bring a small saucepan of water to a boil over high heat. Add the rice noodles, remove from the heat, and let stand until soft, about 10 minutes. Meanwhile, prepare the mangoes, avocados, and cucumber as directed and put in separate bowls. Stack the lettuce leaves and cut into long, narrow strips. Put in a bowl.

**2  MAKE THE ROLLS**

Fill a wide, shallow bowl with hot water and set it on your work surface. Line up the mango, avocado, cucumber, lettuce, and noodle bowls alongside. Slip a rice paper round into the hot water, submerge it for a few seconds, then allow the excess water to drip off and lay it flat on the work surface. (It will continue to soften for a minute or two.) Line up a horizontal row of each of the ingredients from the bowls along the bottom third of the rice paper sheet. Sprinkle evenly with some cilantro and mint.

Fold the bottom edge of the wrapper up and over the filling, pulling it snugly into an even cylinder. Fold the open right side over the filling, then the left. Now, pressing the wrapper tightly over the filling, roll it away from you into a snug cylinder. Set the roll aside, seam side down, and cover with a damp paper towel. Repeat with the remaining filling ingredients and wrappers, keeping the finished rolls covered with a damp paper towel so they don't dry out.

**3  CUT & SERVE THE ROLLS**

To serve, cut each roll in half on the diagonal and arrange the rolls on a platter. Serve with your choice of dipping sauce.

¼ lb (about ½ package) very thin dried rice stick noodles

2 firm but ripe mangoes, peeled, pitted, and thinly sliced (see page 65)

2 firm but ripe avocados, halved, pitted, peeled, and thinly sliced (see page 65)

1 English cucumber, cut into matchsticks

1 small head butter or romaine lettuce, end trimmed and leaves separated

12 rice paper rounds, each 8½ inches in diameter

½ cup firmly packed fresh cilantro leaves

¼ cup thinly sliced fresh mint leaves

Asian Dipping Sauce (page 122) or Peanut Sauce (page 122)

# HOW TO ROLL
# A SUMMER ROLL

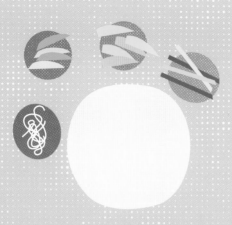

**1**

Dip the rice paper round
in a shallow bowl
of hot water.

**2**

Place the round on a clean
work surface, with bowls
of fillings nearby.

**3**

Line up rows of ingredients
in a bundle on the bottom
third of the round.

**4**

Fold the bottom edge
of the rice paper over
the filling.

**5**

Press the ingredients tightly
toward the bottom of the
roll to create a cylinder.

**6**

Fold the right side of the
round over the filling.

**7**

Fold the left side of the
round over the filling.

**8**

Pulling gently on the
cylinder to keep it tight,
roll up the rice paper roll.

**9**

Cut each roll in half on
the diagonal and serve.

# CHICKEN POTPIES

For an easy short-cut, substitute purchased pie dough for the homemade variety. Egg mixed with cream will make a shiny glaze on either one.

**1 MAKE THE PASTRY DOUGH**

Make the pastry dough and refrigerate as directed. If using store-bought pastry dough, keep refrigerated until needed.

**2 MAKE THE FILLING**

Preheat the oven to 375°F. In a large frying pan over medium-high heat, warm 1 tablespoon of the butter and the oil. Add the onion and cook, stirring often, until soft, about 8 minutes. Add the broccoli, carrots, garlic, and sage and season well with salt and pepper. Cook, stirring often, until the broccoli is bright green, about 2 minutes. Transfer to a large bowl. Return the pan to medium-high heat, add the remaining 3 tablespoons butter and the flour and cook, stirring, for 1 minute. Stir in the broth and the half-and-half. Bring to a simmer and cook, stirring often, until thickened, about 5 minutes. Remove from the heat, add the cooked chicken, then stir into the vegetable mixture. Season with salt and pepper.

**3 ASSEMBLE THE POTPIES**

Have ready six 4½-inch ramekins or similar baking dishes. Using a rolling pin, roll out one dough disk on a lightly floured work surface into a 10-inch round. Cut out 3 rounds about ¼ inch larger than the ramekins. Repeat with the remaining dough disk to make 6 rounds. Cut a small slit in the center of each round to vent the steam. Divide the chicken mixture evenly among the ramekins. Place a dough round over each ramekin, pressing against the rim to seal.

**4 BAKE & SERVE THE POTPIES**

Carefully transfer the ramekins to a rimmed baking sheet. Using a pastry brush, brush the top of each pie with the egg glaze. Bake until the crust is golden brown, 20–25 minutes. Remove from the oven and let cool for 5 minutes, then serve.

Double-Crust Flaky Pie Pastry (page 125) or store-bought refrigerated rolled pie crusts for 2 standard pies

4 tablespoons unsalted butter

1 tablespoon olive oil

½ yellow onion, chopped

2 cups small broccoli florets

2 carrots, peeled and sliced

2 cloves garlic, minced

5 fresh sage leaves, chopped

Salt and freshly ground pepper

¼ cup all-purpose flour

2 cups chicken broth

½ cup half-and-half

3 cups diced Cooked Chicken (page 122)

1 egg mixed with 1 tablespoon heavy cream, for glaze

» THIS DECORATIVE
pastry edge is made by
trimming each dough
round with a fluted pastry
wheel or the tip of a spoon
before topping the dishes.

# SPIRALIZED ZUCCHINI, YELLOW SQUASH & CARROT PASTA

A spiralizer makes quick work of transforming these raw veggies into long, curly "noodles." Ask an adult to help you set it up with the correct blade, if it seems tricky. Don't add the regular spaghetti if you would like to keep it gluten-free.

## 1 SPIRALIZE THE VEGETABLES

Bring a large pot of salted water to a boil over high heat. Meanwhile, set up the spiralizer, fitting it with the fine shredder blade. Trim off both ends of the carrot, zucchini, and yellows quashes. Peel the carrot. Spiralize the carrot into long, round, thin strands following the manufacturer's instructions. Repeat with the zucchini and summer squashes. (If you don't have a spiralizer, you can use a julienne peeler. When cutting the zucchini and yellow squashes, cut only the outer parts, rotating each squash a quarter turn when you reach the seedy center.) Place the zucchini and yellow squashes in a serving bowl and set aside. Discard the center seedy portions of each squash, or reserve for another use.

## 2 COOK THE SPAGHETTI & CARROT

When the water is boiling, add the spaghetti and carrot and stir gently. Cook until the spaghetti is al dente, 6–8 minutes or according to the package directions. Using a big measuring cup, carefully scoop about 1 cup of the cooking water from the pot and set aside. Drain the spaghetti and carrot in a colander set in the sink.

## 3 TOSS THE PASTA WITH THE SAUCE & SERVE

Immediately transfer the spaghetti and carrot to the serving bowl with the squashes and toss to mix and wilt the squash strands slightly. Drizzle with the olive oil, add the butter, and sprinkle with ¼ cup of the Parmesan. Toss until well mixed, stirring in a little of the pasta water if the mixture seems dry. Season with salt and pepper. Sprinkle evenly with the remaining Parmesan. Serve hot.

1 large carrot

1 large zucchini

2 small crookneck or yellow summer squashes

7 oz spaghetti noodles

2 tablespoons garlic-infused olive oil

2 tablespoons unsalted butter

½ cup freshly grated Parmesan cheese

Salt and freshly ground pepper

# SNACKS

# SUSHI HAND ROLLS

Cone-shaped sushi hand rolls, called *temaki*, are an easy way to get started making sushi. You may need to make a trip to a Japanese market for the nori, paper-thin, crisp sheets of dried seaweed with a mild and grassy taste.

**1 MAKE THE SEASONED RICE**

In a small saucepan over low heat, combine the vinegar, sugar, and salt. Heat, stirring, until the sugar and salt dissolve, about 2 minutes. Remove from the heat. Put the hot cooked rice into a large baking dish and use a wooden spatula to spread it out evenly. Slowly pour `kitchen towel and set aside at room temperature for up to 6 hours.

**2 ASSEMBLE THE HAND ROLLS**

In a small bowl, combine the vinegar with 2 tablespoons water. Place 1 piece of nori shiny side down on a clean, dry work surface with a long side closest to you. Scoop about ¼ cup of seasoned rice onto the left third of the nori. Lightly moisten your fingers with the vinegar-water mixture and gently flatten the rice, leaving the edges and corners uncovered. Lightly sprinkle the rice with ½ teaspoon sesame seeds and place a few pieces of cucumber, carrot, and avocado diagonally on the rice, angled from the bottom right of the rice to the far left corner of the nori. Lift the bottom left corner of the nori, bring it up over the fillings, and begin rolling, forming a point at the bottom right edge of the rice; keep rolling until the nori forms a cone around the fillings. Very lightly moisten the seam with the vinegar-water mixture to seal it. Set the hand roll on a platter. Repeat with the remaining ingredients.

**3 SERVE THE HAND ROLLS**

Serve the hand rolls with soy sauce and pickled ginger, if desired.

FOR THE RICE

2 tablespoons rice vinegar

1½ tablespoons sugar

1½ teaspoons salt

1½ cups Steamed Short-Grain White Rice, hot (page 123)

1 teaspoon rice vinegar

3 sheets nori, each about 7 by 8 inches, cut crosswise in half

1 tablespoon toasted sesame seeds

½ English cucumber, peeled and cut into matchsticks

1 carrot, peeled and cut into matchsticks

1 avocado, halved, pitted, peeled, and thinly sliced (see page 65)

Soy sauce and pickled ginger for serving (optional)

**»** VEGGIE SUSHI
takes on a new form
in these easy hand rolls.
Drizzle a little soy sauce
on top before taking a bite
for a hit of salty flavor.

# BACON DEVILED EGGS

It is easiest to remove the shells from hard-boiled eggs that are not super fresh and are completely cold before you try to peel them.

### 1 BOIL THE EGGS

Gently place the eggs in a saucepan. Add water to cover by about 2 inches. Place the pan on the stove top over high heat and bring the water to a boil. Reduce the heat to low and simmer, uncovered, for 10 minutes. Using a slotted spoon, transfer the eggs to a colander and place under cold running water until cool.

### 2 PEEL THE EGGS

Lightly tap an egg on all sides on a countertop until it is covered with cracks. Starting from the large end, carefully peel the egg. Repeat with the remaining eggs. Cut each egg in half lengthwise. Using the tip of a spoon, pry the yolk out of each half, dropping the yolks into a small bowl. Place the whites, hollow side up, on a serving plate.

### 3 FILL THE EGGS

Add the mayonnaise and mustard to the bowl with the yolks. Using a fork, mash and mix to form a paste. Season with salt and white pepper. Spoon the yolk mixture into the egg white halves, dividing it evenly and mounding it in the center. Alternatively, spoon the yolk mixture into a pastry bag fitted with a large plain or star tip and pipe the mixture into the whites.

### 4 SERVE THE DEVILED EGGS

Arrange the deviled eggs on the serving plate. Sprinkle the bacon over the eggs, and serve.

6 large eggs

3 tablespoons mayonnaise

2 teaspoons Dijon mustard

Salt and ground white pepper

2 slices fried bacon (page 43), crumbled

# JUMBO PRETZEL NUGGETS

Just like big ballpark pretzels, these chewy, two-bite nuggets are best when they are fresh and hot. Twist the dough into regular jumbo-size pretzels, if you prefer.

**1** **MAKE THE DOUGH**

In a stand mixer, stir together the warm water, yeast, and sugar. Let stand until foamy, about 10 minutes. Add the olive oil, flour, and salt. Attach the dough hook to the mixer and knead the dough on medium-low speed until smooth, about 10 minutes. Shape the dough into a ball, place in a bowl, and cover the bowl tightly with plastic wrap. Let the dough rise until doubled in size, about 1 hour.

**2** **SHAPE THE PRETZELS**

Preheat the oven to 450°F. Line 2 rimmed baking sheets with parchment paper, then brush the paper with canola oil. Dump the dough onto a lightly floured surface and cut it into 12 equal pieces. Roll each piece into a 1 x 6-inch stick. Cut each stick into 2 or 3 pieces and place, not touching, on the prepared baking sheets.

**3** **BOIL THE PRETZELS**

Fill a large, wide saucepan with the cold water. Stir in the baking soda and bring to a boil over high heat. Gently drop 10 or so dough pieces into the boiling water (without crowding) and boil, turning once with a slotted spoon, for just under 1 minute. Using the spoon, return the boiled pretzel nuggets, top side up, to a prepared baking sheet. Repeat with the remaining dough pieces.

**4** **BAKE THE PRETZELS**

Sprinkle the coarse salt evenly over the pretzels. Bake until golden brown, about 10 minutes.

**5** **SERVE THE PRETZELS**

Meanwhile, make the dip: In a small serving bowl, stir together the honey and mustard, mixing well. Transfer the baked pretzels to a serving dish. Serve warm with the dip alongside.

FOR THE DOUGH

1 cup warm water (105°–115°F)

1 package (2¼ teaspoons) active dry yeast

1 tablespoon sugar

3 tablespoons olive oil

3¼ cups all-purpose flour, plus more for dusting

1 teaspoon salt

Canola oil for brushing

7 cups cold water

⅓ cup baking soda

Coarse sea salt for sprinkling

FOR THE SWEET MUSTARD DIP

⅓ cup honey

1 cup brown mustard

# BRUSCHETTA TRIPLE PLAY

Fresh tomato, basil, and garlic is the classic preparation for these garlic-rubbed toasts. Here, you can go the traditional route, or select one of two more toppings.

**1** **TOAST THE BREAD**

Using a toaster or the broiler, toast the bread slices on both sides until golden. Rub the cut side of a garlic half over one side of each toast. Using a pastry brush, brush the garlic-rubbed sides with oil.

**2** **TOP THE BREAD SLICES**

Top the toasts with your choice of toppings:

**NECTARINE, BURRATA & ARUGULA** Cut 2 nectarines in half, remove the pit, then cut into slices. Spread 2 oz burrata cheese on the toasts, dividing it evenly, then top evenly with the nectarine slices. Sprinkle ½ cup of baby arugula leaves over the toasts, then drizzle evenly with olive oil. Season to taste with salt and pepper.

**CHERRY TOMATO, BASIL & GARLIC** In a bowl, mix 1 tablespoon balsamic vinegar with a pinch each of salt and pepper. Whisk in 3 tablespoons olive oil. Stir in ½ cup small, fresh basil leaves. Cut 2 cups mixed yellow and cherry tomatoes into halves, add to the vinaigrette, and toss to mix. Spoon the tomatoes over the toasts, dividing evenly.

**CUCUMBER, HERBS & CREAM CHEESE** In a small bowl, mix 6 oz cream cheese with 1 tablespoon thinly sliced fresh chives or dill until evenly blended. Season with salt and pepper and mix again. Spread the cream cheese on the toasts, dividing it evenly. Cut ½ English cucumber into very thin slices. Arrange the cucumber slices over the cream cheese, dividing them evenly. Garnish with a sprinkling of extra chives or dill.

6 slices country-style French or Italian bread, about ¾ inch thick

1 clove garlic, cut lengthwise in half

Olive oil for brushing

# SWEET & SALTY SEEDS

makes
**4-6**
servings

Like pepitas and sunflower seeds, pine nuts are seeds too. Despite their name, pine nuts are actually the edible seeds from pinecones. Like all seeds and nuts, they have a tough outer shell that must be removed before they can be eaten.

**1  MIX THE SEEDS**

Preheat the oven to 350°F. Line a rimmed baking sheet with parchment paper. Put the butter in a microwave-safe bowl large enough to hold all the seeds and nuts. Microwave on high power until melted, 10-15 seconds. Add the honey and cinnamon and stir until blended. Add the pumpkin seeds, pine nuts, and sunflower seeds and stir until evenly coated.

**2  BAKE THE SEEDS**

Spread the seeds in a single layer on the prepared baking sheet. (If you are having trouble spreading the seeds, moisten your hands with water and try again.) Bake just until golden, 5-6 minutes.

**3  BREAK UP THE CLUSTERS**

Remove the pan from the oven. Carefully transfer the parchment paper holding the nuts to a wire rack. When cool enough to handle, break up the seed clusters with your hands and transfer to a serving bowl. Sprinkle to taste with salt and serve. Store leftover seeds in a covered container for up to 1 week.

1 tablespoon unsalted
butter, melted

2 tablespoons honey

¾ teaspoon ground cinnamon

¾ cup pepitas (pumpkin seeds)

½ cup pine nuts

¼ cup sunflower seeds

Kosher salt for sprinkling

# DRESSED UP POPCORN

With its soft exterior and all its nooks and crannies, popcorn can take on any flavor—sweet, salty, or savory—making it an exceptionally tasty and versatile snack. Toss it with seasonings when hot and just popped for the best results.

**1** **POP THE CORN**

In a large, heavy-bottomed pan with a tight-fitting lid, warm the oil over medium heat. Add the popcorn and cover the pan. Leave the pan untouched until you hear the first few pops, then shake the pan and continue to cook, shaking the pan every 20 seconds or so, until the popping slows way, way down, about 6 minutes. Remove from the heat.

**2** **DRESS THE POPCORN**

While the popcorn is still hot, toss it with your choice of the following flavor combinations:

**RANCH** In a large bowl, stir together 2 tablespoons *each* melted unsalted butter and freshly grated Parmesan cheese; ½ teaspoon each onion powder, dried dill, and salt; and ¼ teaspoon garlic powder. Add the hot popcorn and toss to mix.

**TRAIL MIX** In a large bowl, toss together 2 tablespoons melted unsalted butter and the hot popcorn. Add ½ cup each dried cranberries and salted peanuts, ¼ cup chocolate chips (any kind), and 2 tablespoons maple syrup and toss to mix.

**CHEESY** In a large bowl, toss together 3 tablespoons melted butter and 1 teaspoon salt. Add the hot popcorn and toss to coat evenly. Sprinkle 1 cup grated Parmesan cheese over the buttered popcorn and toss to mix.

2 tablespoons canola oil

½ cup unpopped popcorn

Sweet & Salty
Seeds (page 88)

Peanutty Rice
Puffs (page 93)

Trail Mix Popcorn
(page 89)

Root Veggie Chips
(page 92)

Jumbo Pretzel Nuggets
(page 85)

Ranch Popcorn
(page 89)

» SUPER
DELICIOUS
SNACKS

# ROOT VEGGIE CHIPS

Any kind of root vegetable works well in this recipe. In addition to the sweet potato, parsnips, or rutabaga suggested here, you can experiment with carrots, turnips, beets, or even ordinary potatoes.

**1 SLICE THE SWEET POTATO**

Preheat the oven to 400°F. Line a rimmed baking sheet with parchment paper. Using a vegetable peeler, peel the sweet potato. Ask an adult to help you slice the sweet potato. Using a food processor fitted with the thinnest slicing disk, a mandoline, or a sharp knife, slice the sweet potato crosswise into very thin rounds no more than ⅛ inch thick.

**2 COAT WITH OIL**

Put the slices in a big bowl and drizzle with the oil. Using your hands, gently toss the slices until they are evenly coated. Lay the sweet potato slices in a single layer, overlapping them as little as possible, on the prepared baking sheet. Use a pastry brush to spread the oil remaining in the bowl on any uncoated slices.

**3 BAKE THE CHIPS**

Bake the slices for 10 minutes. Remove the baking sheet from the oven and, using a wide metal spatula, turn over all the slices. Sprinkle the slices evenly with ¼ teaspoon salt. Return the baking sheet to the oven and continue to bake until the slices are dry and some are lightly browned, about 10 minutes longer. Check often during the last few minutes of baking to make sure they do not burn.

**4 SALT & SERVE**

Remove the baking sheet from the oven and carefully slide the chips into a serving bowl. Sprinkle with a little more salt and serve warm.

1 small sweet potato,
2 parsnips, or 1 rutabaga,
about ¼ lb

1 tablespoon olive oil

Salt

# PEANUTTY RICE PUFFS

Be sure to use the plump kernels of puffed rice cereal, rather than crunchier crisped rice cereal, for these featherlight puffs. Store any leftovers in an airtight container at room temperature for up to 3 days—if they last that long!

**1 MIX THE INGREDIENTS**

In a saucepan over medium heat, combine the agave nectar and brown sugar. Heat, stirring, until the mixture begins to boil and the brown sugar dissolves, 2-3 minutes. Remove from the heat. Add the peanut butter and stir until blended and smooth. Add the cereal and stir gently until evenly coated. Set the mixture aside until cool enough to handle, about 5 minutes.

**2 MAKE THE PUFFS**

Lightly grease a rimmed baking sheet with butter. Set a bowl filled with water on the work surface. Dampen your hands with a little water to prevent sticking as you shape the balls. Using a spoon, scoop up 1 tablespoon or so of the cereal mixture and use your hands to press it into a ball 1½ inches in diameter (just a bit smaller than a golf ball). Place the ball on the prepared baking sheet. Continue to scoop and mold the remaining cereal mixture into balls, dampening your hands as needed and placing them evenly apart on the baking sheet. You should have about 20 balls.

**3 CHILL & SERVE**

Place the baking sheet in the refrigerator and chill the balls until set, 5-10 minutes. Remove the balls from the refrigerator, transfer them to a serving plate or bowl, and serve.

¼ cup agave nectar or honey

2 tablespoons firmly packed golden brown sugar

¼ cup natural creamy peanut butter or other nut butter

1¾ cups puffed rice cereal

Unsalted butter for greasing

# DESSERTS

# UNICORN MARBLE BUNDT CAKE

Unicorns are all about multicolored fantasy, and the concept finds its way into cakes and cookies in a rainbow of pastel hues with lots of candy sprinkles too.

**1 MAKE THE BATTER**

Preheat the oven to 325°F. Grease a 10-inch Bundt pan with butter, then dust with flour, tapping out the excess. In a bowl, stir together the flour, baking soda, and salt. In another bowl, beat the butter and sugar with an electric mixer on medium-high speed until fluffy, 5–7 minutes. Beat in the eggs, one at a time. Add the vanilla and beat until blended. With the mixer on low speed, add the flour mixture in three additions alternately with the sour cream in two additions, beating just until blended after each addition.

**2 MARBLE THE CAKE BATTER**

Scoop a heaping 1 cup of the batter into a small bowl. Then scoop a heaping 1 cup of the batter into another small bowl. Transfer the remaining batter to the prepared Bundt pan, spreading it evenly. Add 8 drops of red food coloring to the batter in one small bowl, and 8 drops of blue food coloring to the batter in the other small bowl. Using a rubber spatula, gently fold the food coloring into each bowl of batter. Spoon the red batter in blobs over the plain batter in the Bundt pan, then spoon the blue batter in blobs between the red batter blobs. To marble the batter, draw a wooden skewer or chopstick through the batter in a series of figure eights.

**3 BAKE THE CAKE**

Bake the cake until a toothpick inserted near the center comes out clean, 1¼ to 1½ hours. Let cool in the pan on a wire rack for 10 minutes. Invert the pan onto the rack, lift off the pan, and let cool.

**4 ICE THE CAKE**

Drizzle the icing over the cake so it runs down the sides. Scatter candy sprinkles and confetti on top. Cut into slices and serve.

FOR THE CAKE

1 cup unsalted butter, at room temperature, plus more for preparing the pan

3 cups cake flour, plus more for preparing the pan

¼ teaspoon baking soda

¼ teaspoon salt

2½ cups granulated sugar

6 large eggs, at room temperature

2 teaspoons pure vanilla extract

1 cup sour cream

Red and blue food coloring or colorings of choice

Vanilla Cake Icing (page 125)

Candy sprinkles and confetti for garnish

**» BAKE PIE POPS** with sticks at intervals between the pies or pointed towards the pan center to prevent the stick ends from overbrowning.

# BERRY PIE POPS

Cute and clever, these pie pops are just a few bites each. Blueberries (and blackberries too!) get plump and juicy when baked between layers of pastry.

**1 MAKE THE PASTRY DOUGH**

Make the pastry dough and refrigerate as directed. If using store-bought pastry dough, keep refrigerated until needed. Preheat the oven to 375°F. Line a rimmed baking sheet with parchment paper. Submerge 8 wooden ice pop sticks in a glass of water.

**2 MAKE THE FILLING**

In a bowl, mix the blueberries, sugar, flour, and lemon juice. Using a fork, crush half of the berries to release their juices. Set aside.

**3 ROLL & CUT THE PASTRY**

Using a rolling pin, roll out the dough on a lightly floured work surface into thin 18-inch rounds. Using a 3-inch round biscuit cutter, cut out as many rounds as possible and refrigerate until ready to use. Gather the scraps and knead briefly, then roll and cut out more rounds. You should have 16 rounds total. Cut a small vent in the center of 8 of the rounds and refrigerate until ready to use.

**4 SHAPE THE PIE POPS**

Place 8 uncut rounds on the prepared baking sheet. Using a small pastry brush, brush the edge of each round with the egg white. Dry the ice pop sticks with a paper towel and place one into the center of each round. Spoon about 2 teaspoons of the berry mixture onto the center of each round, cover with a vented round, and use the tines of a fork to press around the edge of each round to secure the seal. Brush with the egg white, then sprinkle evenly with sugar.

**5 BAKE THE PIE POPS**

Bake the pie pops until golden and crisp, 18–20 minutes. Let cool on wire racks. Serve warm or at room temperature.

Double-Crust Flaky Pie Pastry (page 125) or store-bought rolled pie crusts for 2 standard pies, refrigerated

FOR THE BERRY FILLING
1 cup fresh blueberries or blackberries

2 tablespoons sugar

1½ teaspoons all-purpose flour

1 teaspoon fresh lemon juice

All-purpose flour for dusting

1 egg white, lightly beaten

Sugar for sprinkling

# SUMMERY PEACH CRISP

An easy mixture of sugary oats and pecans bakes up nice and crunchy in the oven—the perfect topping for a sweet and juicy mixture of fresh peaches.

**1 MIX THE TOPPING**

Preheat the oven to 375°F. In a small bowl, mix the oats, brown sugar, ¼ cup of the flour, the nuts, ½ teaspoon of the cinnamon, the nutmeg, and salt. Using your fingertips, rub the butter into the oat mixture until well blended and the mixture is crumbly.

**2 PEEL THE PEACHES**

Bring a large pot of water to a boil over high heat. Fill a large bowl with ice-cold water and set it nearby. Using a slotted spoon, lower the peaches into the boiling water and blanch for 30 seconds, then transfer to the ice water until cool. Remove the peaches from the water and, using your fingers, peel off and discard the skins.

**3 MAKE THE PEACH FILLING**

Cut the peaches in half and remove the pits. Place each half cut side down and cut lengthwise into slices. Put the slices in a bowl. Add the granulated sugar, the remaining ¼ cup flour, and the remaining ½ teaspoon cinnamon and stir to mix well.

**4 LAYER THE INGREDIENTS**

Divide the peach mixture evenly among eight 1-cup gratin dishes or one 9 x 12-inch baking dish, spreading it out evenly. Scatter the topping evenly over the peaches. If using individual gratin dishes, put the gratin dishes on a large rimmed baking sheet.

**5 BAKE THE CRISP**

Bake the crisp until the juices are bubbling and the topping is browned, 30-35 minutes. Let cool slightly. If serving the large crisp, scoop out portions onto individual plates. Serve warm or at room temperature, accompanied by vanilla ice cream, if desired.

½ cup old-fashioned rolled oats

½ cup firmly packed golden brown sugar

½ cup all-purpose flour

¼ cup almonds or pecans, finely chopped

1 teaspoon ground cinnamon

¼ teaspoon ground nutmeg

¼ teaspoon salt

6 tablespoons butter, at room temperature

4 peaches, about 2 lb total

⅓ cup granulated sugar

Vanilla ice cream for serving (optional)

# INDIVIDUAL APPLE GALETTES

The word *galette* is French and refers to a free-form tart. The sweet, imperfectly shaped crusts framing these apple tarts make them charming and delicious.

**1** **MAKE THE PASTRY DOUGH**

Make the pastry dough and refrigerate as directed. If using store-bought pastry dough, keep refrigerated until needed. Line 2 rimmed baking sheets with parchment paper.

**2** **MAKE THE FILLING**

In a large bowl, toss together the apples, lemon zest, lemon juice, granulated sugar, cinnamon, and salt, coating the apples evenly.

**3** **FORM THE GALETTES**

Place 1 dough disk on a lightly floured surface and cut into 3 equal pieces. Using a rolling pin, roll out each piece into a round about ⅛ inch thick. Transfer the dough rounds to a prepared baking sheet. Repeat with the second dough disk, transferring the rounds to the second prepared baking sheet. Divide the apples evenly among the dough rounds, spreading them into an even layer and leaving a 1-inch border uncovered on the edge. Fold the edge of the dough up and over the apples, loosely pleating the dough and leaving the center uncovered. Refrigerate for about 30 minutes. After 15 minutes, preheat the oven to 400°F.

**4** **BAKE THE GALETTES**

Bake the galettes, rotating the pans halfway through baking, until the crust is golden brown and the apples are tender, about 40 minutes. Let the galettes cool on the pans on a wire rack. Serve warm or at room temperature. Accompany each galette with a scoop of ice cream, if desired.

Double-Crust Flaky Pie Pastry (page 125) or store-bought rolled pie crusts for 2 standard pies, refrigerated

4 apples, such as pippin, Granny Smith, Crispin, or Pink Lady, peeled, halved, cored, and sliced ¼ inch thick

Grated zest of 1 lemon

1 tablespoon fresh lemon juice

¼ cup granulated sugar

½ tsp ground cinnamon

Pinch of salt

Caramel or vanilla ice cream for serving (optional)

# WATERMELON-LIME ICE POPS

The thirst-quenching Mexican drink called *agua fresca*, a mixture of fruit, water, and sugar, is the inspiration for these colorful layered ice pops. Make them on a summer morning and enjoy them in the hot afternoon.

**1** **MAKE THE WATERMELON LAYER**

Scoop the flesh from the watermelon and remove any seeds. Chop the watermelon flesh; you should have about 4 cups. Transfer to a blender or food processor, add the sugar, lime juice, and salt, and blend until smooth. Using a spoon, stir in the chocolate chips.

Divide the watermelon mixture evenly among 8-10 ice pop molds, filling them three-fourths full. Freeze until the mixture is partially frozen, about 1 hour.

**2** **MAKE THE LIME LAYER**

In a clean blender or food processor, combine the lime zest and juice, sugar, and water. Add the green food coloring and blend until smooth. Refrigerate until ready to use.

**3** **FINISH ASSEMBLING THE ICE POPS**

When the watermelon layer is partially frozen, divide the lime mixture evenly among the ice pop molds, distributing it evenly. If using ice pop sticks, insert them at this point. Cover and freeze ice pops until solid, at least 3 hours or up to 3 days.

FOR THE WATERMELON LAYER

½ small watermelon, about 2 lb

3 tablespoons superfine sugar

2 tablespoons fresh lime juice

Pinch of salt

¼ cup mini semisweet chocolate chips

FOR THE LIME LAYER

½ teaspoon grated lime zest

2 tablespoons fresh lime juice

2½ tablespoons superfine sugar

⅓ cup water

2 or 3 drops green food coloring

flower candy
sprinkles

crushed
dehydrated
& fresh
strawberries

candy
confetti

silver stars

crushed graham
crackers &
chocolate chips

bananas, peanuts
& maraschino
cherry

# CUPCAKES GALORE

The sky is the limit when it comes to decorating cupcakes. You can stick with vanilla cake and icing (as here), add flavor or color to the icing (next page), or switch to chocolate cake and frosting (page 110). Also, get creative with all your cupcake toppings. Sprinkles and confetti are natural choices, but you can also try fresh and dehydrated fruits, crushed cookies, and specialty sprinkles.

**1 MAKE THE CUPCAKE BATTER**

Preheat the oven to 350°F. Line a standard 12-cup muffin pan with paper liners. In a bowl, stir together the flour, baking powder, and salt. In a large bowl, using a handheld mixer or a stand mixer fitted with the paddle attachment, beat together the butter, sugar, and vanilla on medium speed until creamy, about 3 minutes. Add the eggs, one at a time, beating well after each addition. Stop the mixer and scrape down the sides of the bowl with a rubber spatula. With the mixer on low speed, beat in the flour mixture in three additions alternately with the milk in two additions, beginning and ending with the flour mixture and beating just until blended after each addition. Stop the mixer and scrape down the sides of the bowl with the spatula as needed.

**2 BAKE THE CUPCAKES**

Divide the batter evenly among the prepared muffin cups, filling each cup about three-fourths full. Bake until golden and a toothpick inserted into the center of a cupcake comes out clean, 17–20 minutes. Let cool in the pan on a wire rack for 5 minutes, then remove the cupcakes from the pan and let cool completely.

FOR THE CUPCAKES

1½ cups all-purpose flour

2 teaspoons baking powder

Large pinch of salt

½ cup unsalted butter, at room temperature

1 cup sugar

1 teaspoon pure vanilla extract

2 large eggs, at room temperature

¾ cup whole milk, at room temperature

*Continued on page 106 »*

» *Continued from page 105*

## 3 FROST THE CUPCAKES

To make the frosting, in a bowl, using the handheld mixer or the stand mixer fitted with the paddle attachment, beat together the butter, cream, vanilla, and salt on medium speed until creamy and smooth, about 2 minutes. Add the powdered sugar and beat until smooth. Spread the frosting on the cooled cupcakes. Serve at room temperature.

### VARIATIONS

**Tinted Frosting**: Make the frosting as directed, then beat in a food coloring of choice, a drop at a time, until the desired color is achieved.

**Vanilla & Chocolate Marble Cupcakes**: In a small bowl, stir together ¼ cup hot water and ¼ cup unsweetened cocoa powder. Make the vanilla cupcake batter as directed. Spoon 1¾ cups of the batter into a bowl and stir in the cocoa mixture until blended. Working with 1 prepared muffin cup at a time, spoon enough of the vanilla batter into one side of the cup to fill it almost halfway. Then spoon enough of the chocolate batter into the other side of the cup to fill it about four-fifths full. (You may have enough batter left over for an extra cupcake or two.) Using a knife, draw a circle through the batter in each cup and bake the cupcakes as directed.

### FOR THE FROSTING

6 tablespoons unsalted butter, at room temperature

1 tablespoon heavy cream

1 teaspoon pure vanilla extract

⅛ teaspoon salt

1⅔ cups powdered sugar

# CHEWY OATMEAL COOKIES

Remove these palm-size cookies from the oven when the edges are just starting to brown for the perfect chewy consistency. Store any leftovers in an airtight container at room temperature for up to 5 days—though they probably won't be around that long.

## 1 MIX THE COOKIE DOUGH

Preheat the oven to 350°F. Line 2 baking sheets with parchment paper. In a bowl, sift together the flour, baking soda, cinnamon, and salt. In a large bowl, using a handheld mixer or a stand mixer fitted with the paddle attachment, beat together the butter and both sugars on medium-high speed until combined. Add the eggs and vanilla and beat until well blended. Reduce the speed to low, add the flour mixture and oats, and beat just until incorporated. Using a spatula or wooden spoon, gently stir in the raisins.

## 2 BAKE THE COOKIES

Using a tablespoon, scoop up round, heaping spoonfuls of dough and place them on the prepared pans, spacing them well apart. Bake the cookies, rotating the pans halfway through baking, until golden brown, about 15 minutes. Let the cookies cool on the pans on wire racks for 5 minutes, then, using a metal spatula, transfer them to the racks to cool completely.

1½ cups all-purpose flour

1 teaspoon baking soda

2 teaspoons ground cinnamon

½ teaspoon salt

¾ cup unsalted butter, at room temperature

1 cup firmly packed golden brown sugar

½ cup granulated sugar

2 large eggs

2 teaspoons pure vanilla extract

2¼ cups old-fashioned rolled oats

1 cup golden or black raisins, dried currants, or chocolate chips (any kind)

# ICE CREAM DREAM

Start with a good vanilla base and ice cream can be varied to take on a mix of flavors and add-ins according to your own preferences—making any ice cream you create a dream come true. Creativity can come into play when serving too. Try ice cream sandwiches dipped in chocolate or scoops atop soda in floats.

**1** **MAKE THE ICE CREAM BASE**
In a large bowl, whisk together the cream and milk. Add the sugar and whisk until completely dissolved, 3–4 minutes. Stir in the vanilla. Cover and refrigerate for at least 3 hours or up to 24 hours.

**2** **FREEZE THE ICE CREAM BASE**
Pour the ice cream base into an ice cream maker and freeze according to the manufacturer's instructions. Transfer to a freezer-safe container and freeze until firm, at least 3 hours or up to 3 days.

2 cups cold heavy cream

1 cup cold whole milk

¾ cup sugar, preferably superfine

1 tablespoon pure vanilla extract

### VARIATIONS

**Mint Chip:** Substitute 1½ teaspoons peppermint extract for the vanilla. Add ¾ cup semisweet chocolate chips to the ice cream maker during the last 5 minutes of freezing time.

**Cookies & Cream:** Add ¾ cup coarsely chopped Oreos to the ice cream maker during the last 5 minutes of freezing time.

**Strawberry:** Reduce the vanilla extract to 1 teaspoon. Add 2 cups strawberries, hulled and coarsely chopped, to the ice cream maker during the last minute of freezing time.

### SERVING IDEA

**Ice Cream Sandwich:** Soften the ice cream at room temperature. Sandwich each scoop between two oatmeal cookies (page 107). Melt 1 cup chocolate chips with 1 tablespoon vegetable shortening in the microwave for 50 seconds, then stir until smooth. Dip sandwiches in the chocolate, then into a dish of candy confetti. Freeze until firm.

# ULTRA CHOCOLATE CAKE

Dense chocolate cake richly swept with mounds of fudgy chocolate frosting—this towering double-layer cake is a favorite among chocoholics everywhere. Serve each slice with a scoop of vanilla ice cream to complement its richness.

**1 PREPARE THE PANS**

Preheat the oven to 350°F. Butter two 9-inch round cake pans. Line the cake pans with parchment paper cut to fit the bottom exactly. Butter the paper and then sprinkle lightly with flour, tapping out the excess.

**2 MELT THE CHOCOLATE**

Put the unsweetened chocolate in a heatproof bowl and set over (not touching) simmering water in a saucepan. Heat, stirring often, until melted and smooth, about 5 minutes. Remove from the heat and let cool.

**3 MAKE THE CAKE BATTER**

In a bowl, stir together the flour, baking soda, and salt. In a large bowl, using a handheld mixer or a stand mixer fitted with the paddle attachment, beat together the butter and brown and granulated sugars on medium speed until creamy, about 2 minutes. Add the eggs, one at a time, beating well after each addition. Stop the mixer and scrape down the sides of the bowl with a rubber spatula. Add the vanilla and beat on medium speed for 1 minute longer. Add the melted chocolate and beat until evenly blended. With the mixer on low speed, add the flour mixture in three additions alternately with the buttermilk in two additions, beginning and ending with the flour mixture and beating just until blended after each addition. Stop the mixer and scrape down the sides of the bowl with the spatula as needed.

FOR THE CAKE

4 oz unsweetened chocolate, finely chopped

2¼ cups all-purpose flour

1 teaspoon baking soda

¼ teaspoon salt

1 cup unsalted butter, at room temperature

1 cup firmly packed golden brown sugar

¾ cup granulated sugar

4 large eggs, at room temperature

2 teaspoons pure vanilla extract

1 cup low-fat buttermilk, at room temperature

**Chocolate Fudge Frosting (page 125)**

## 4 BAKE THE CAKE LAYERS

Pour the batter into the prepared pans, dividing it evenly. Bake until a toothpick inserted into the center of each cake comes out clean, 30–35 minutes. Transfer the cakes to wire racks and let cool in the pans for 20 minutes. Invert 1 cake layer onto a plate, lift off the pan, peel off the parchment paper, and turn the layer right side up. Repeat with the remaining cake layer. Let the cakes cool completely.

## 5 FROST THE CAKE & SERVE

While the cakes are cooling, make the frosting according to the directions. When the cakes have cooled, place a cake layer, bottom side down, on a cake plate. Scoop about one-third of the frosting onto the center, then, using an icing spatula, spread the frosting evenly over the top. Place the second cake layer, top side down, on top. Spread frosting around the sides of the cake, then frost the top. Cut into wedges and serve.

### VARIATION

**Cupcakes:** Omit the two cake pans. Instead, line 18 muffin cups in two standard 12-cup muffin pans with paper liners. Divide the batter evenly among the prepared muffin cups, filling each cup about three-fourths full. Bake until a toothpick inserted into the center of a cupcake comes out clean, 17–20 minutes. Let cool in the pan on a wire rack for 5 minutes, then remove the cupcakes from the pan and let cool completely.

» **THE CAKE LAYERS** can be baked up to 1 day in advance, well wrapped in plastic wrap, and stored at room temperature before you assemble the cake layers and frost them.

# DECADENT BROWNIES

If the only brownies you have ever baked were from a brownie-mix box, you're in for a treat. Whether you're craving a great chocolaty brownie or one with some sweet bells and whistles, you'll find it here and on the next page.

**1 MAKE THE BROWNIE BATTER**

Preheat the oven to 350°F. Butter a 9 x 13-inch baking pan. In a medium bowl, sift together the flour, baking soda, and salt. Set aside. In a saucepan over medium heat, melt the butter. Remove from the heat and add the chocolate. Let stand for 3 minutes, then whisk until smooth. Whisk in both sugars until blended. Whisk in the eggs, one at a time, then whisk in the corn syrup and vanilla. Add the flour mixture and stir until combined.

**2 BAKE THE BROWNIES**

Spread the batter evenly in the prepared pan. Bake until a toothpick inserted into the center comes out with a few moist crumbs attached, about 25 minutes. Let cool in the pan on a wire rack. Cut into about 12 squares.

¾ cup unsalted butter, plus more for greasing

1 cup all-purpose flour

½ teaspoon baking soda

½ teaspoon sea salt

6 oz unsweetened chocolate, finely chopped

1 cup granulated sugar

1 cup firmly packed golden brown sugar

4 large eggs, at room temperature

¼ cup light corn syrup, honey, or maple syrup

2 teaspoons pure vanilla extract

*Continued on page 114 »*

» *Continued from page 113*

**GRAHAM CRACKER + MARSHMALLOW** Make the brownie batter as directed. Scrape the batter into the prepared pan and spread evenly. Crush 6 graham crackers with your hands and scatter evenly over the top. Place 12 jumbo marshmallows over the graham crackers, spacing them evenly. Bake as directed.

**CARAMEL SAUCE + SEA SALT + MACADAMIA NUT** Make the brownie batter and bake as directed. Before serving, unwrap a 14-oz bag of caramels, put them in a small saucepan, and add ¼ cup milk. Place over medium heat and heat, stirring often, until smooth, about 5 minutes. Stir in 2 tablespoons unsalted butter. Top each brownie with a drizzle of caramel, a sprinkling of flaky sea salt, and a spoonful of chopped toasted macadamia nuts.

**COCONUT FLAKE + CHOCOLATE CHUNK + PECAN** Make the brownie batter as directed. Bake the brownie until just set, 16–18 minutes. Layer 2 cups unsweetened flaked dried coconut and 1 package (11½ oz) semisweet chocolate chunks over the brownie, then pour 1 can (14 fl oz) sweetened condensed milk evenly over the top. Sprinkle evenly with 1 cup chopped pecans. Return the brownie to the oven and continue baking until the topping is lightly browned and a toothpick inserted into the center comes out with a few moist crumbs attached, 15–20 minutes longer.

**PEPPERMINT CRUNCH** Make the brownie batter as directed, but use 2 teaspoons peppermint extract instead of the 2 teaspoons vanilla extract. Scrape the batter into the prepared pan and spread evenly. Place 1 cup of hard, unwrapped peppermint candies into a large, heavy-duty lock-top plastic bag. Seal the bag closed and, using a meat pounder, crush the candies into small pieces. Sprinkle the crushed candies evenly over the brownie batter. Bake as directed.

» MAKE IT A DOUBLE
Baking chocolate that is unsweetened in its raw form can often contribute to the densest chocolate flavor when melted and sweetened for a recipe. For double-chocolate brownies, stir ½ cup semisweet chocolate chips into the batter just before baking.

# MADELEINES

Madeleines are French cake-like cookies baked in a special pan with seashell-shaped molds. Sifting the flour and beating the egg-sugar mixture give the madeleines a wonderful light texture—almost like sponge cake.

**1 PREPARE THE PAN**
Position a rack in the lower third of the oven and preheat the oven to 400°F. Using a pastry brush and 1 tablespoon of the butter, coat the 12 molds of the madeleine pan with a thick layer of butter. Dust the molds with flour, tilting the pan to coat all of the surfaces. Turn the pan upside down over the kitchen sink and tap it gently to knock out the excess flour.

**2 MAKE THE BATTER**
Sift together the flour and baking powder into a bowl. In another bowl, using an electric mixer, beat together the egg and sugar on medium speed for 30 seconds. Increase the speed to high and beat until very thick and quadrupled in bulk, about 10 minutes. Beat in the vanilla. Turn off the mixer. Sprinkle the flour mixture over the egg mixture. Using a rubber spatula, gently fold in the flour mixture, then fold in the remaining 4 tablespoons butter.

**3 BAKE THE MADELEINES**
Scoop a heaping tablespoonful of batter into each mold, filling each one about three-fourths full. Bake until the cookies are golden brown and the tops spring back when lightly touched, 10–12 minutes. Remove the pan from the oven, immediately invert it onto a wire rack, and tap the pan on the rack to release the madeleines. If any of the cookies stick, use a butter knife to loosen the edges, then invert and tap again. Turn the cakes right side up and let cool.

**4 DUST THE MADELEINES WITH SUGAR & SERVE**
Using a fine-mesh sieve or a sifter, dust the madeleines with powdered sugar, then serve.

5 tablespoons unsalted butter, melted and cooled

½ cup cake flour, plus more for dusting the pan

½ teaspoon baking powder

1 large egg

¼ cup granulated sugar

1 teaspoon vanilla extract

Powdered sugar for dusting

**» BAKING TIP**
Also called plaques, madeleine pans typically have 12 shallow molds and come in tinned steel, metal with a nonstick finish, or pliable silicone. If you use a black nonstick madeleine pan, reduce the oven temperature to 375°F or shorten the baking time by a few minutes.

# LATTICED CHERRY PIE

You can pit the cherries with a paring knife, but the job goes more quickly if you have a nifty handheld cherry pitter. Look for one at a kitchen supply store.

**1** **MAKE THE PASTRY DOUGH**

Make the pastry dough and refrigerate as directed. If using store-bought pastry dough, keep refrigerated until needed.

**2** **ROLL OUT THE DOUGH & LINE THE PIE PAN**

Place 1 dough disk on a lightly floured surface; keep the remaining disk in the refrigerator. Using a rolling pin, roll out the dough into a 12-inch round. Fold the dough round in half, then into quarters, and transfer it to a 9-inch pie pan, positioning the point at the center. Unfold the dough, press it into the pan, and trim the edges flush with the pan rim. Place in the freezer for 30 minutes.

**3** **MAKE THE FILLING**

Position a rack in the lower third of the oven and preheat the oven to 400°F. In a large bowl, mix the cherries, sugar, and flour.

**4** **MAKE THE LATTICE TOP**

Place the remaining dough disk on the lightly floured work surface and roll out into round about 11 inches in diameter. Using a small knife or a pastry wheel, cut into strips about 1 inch wide. Remove the pastry shell from the freezer and turn the cherry mixture into it. Weave the strips over the cherry filling to form a lattice (see right). Trim the edges flush with the pan rim and crimp to seal and form an attractive edge. In a small bowl, mix the egg yolk and milk. Using a pastry brush, brush the dough with the egg mixture.

**5** **BAKE & SERVE THE PIE**

Bake the pie until the juices bubble thickly and the crust is golden, 1–1¼ hours. Let cool on a wire rack before serving. Cut into wedges and accompany each slice with a scoop of ice cream.

Double-Crust Flaky Pie Pastry (page 125) or store-bought rolled pie crusts for 2 standard pies

FOR THE FILLING

1¾ lb sweet cherries, such as Royal Ann, Bing, or Rainier, pitted

¾ cup sugar

2 tablespoons all-purpose flour

1 large egg yolk

1 tablespoon whole or low-fat milk

Vanilla ice cream for serving

# HOW TO WEAVE A LATTICE PIE CRUST

**1**

Lay 2 vertical strips about 2 inches apart over the pie center. Lay 1 horizontal strip over the center.

**2**

Place 3 vertical strips on either side of the 2 middle strips, laying them over the center horizontal strip.

**3**

Arrange the vertical strips at even intervals about ½ inch apart.

**4**

Lift the bottom half of the 2 vertical strips on either side of the center one. Lay a horizontal strip on top of the remaining 3 vertical strips.

**5**

Lay the folded strips back down over the new horizontal strip so all strips are ½ inch apart.

**6**

Lift the center and side vertical strips and add a third horizontal strip. Weave the other half of the pie the same way.

# SUGAR COOKIES

Sugar cookies are the perfect blank canvas. Decorate them simply with icing (page 125) or use the dough to make jam hearts or stained glass cookies.

**1 MAKE THE COOKIE DOUGH**

In a bowl, stir together the flour, baking powder, and salt. In a large bowl, using a handheld mixer or a stand mixer fitted with the paddle attachment, beat the butter and granulated sugar on medium speed until well blended, about 1 minute. Beat in the egg and vanilla until combined. Gradually beat in the flour on low speed just until blended, stopping to scrape down the bowl with a rubber spatula if needed. The dough will look lumpy, like moist pebbles. Dump the dough onto a work surface and press into a mound. Divide the dough in half, press each half into a disk, and wrap in plastic wrap. Refrigerate for at least 1 hour or up to overnight.

**2 CUT OUT THE COOKIES**

Preheat the oven to 350°F. Line 2 baking sheets with parchment paper. Place 1 dough disk on a lightly floured work surface and sprinkle it with a little flour. Using a rolling pin, roll out the dough into a round about ¼ inch thick. Sprinkle more flour under and over the dough as needed to keep it from sticking. Using your cookie cutters of choice, cut out as many cookies as possible. Transfer the cookies to the prepared pans, spacing them 1 inch apart. Gather up the dough scraps, press them into a disk, wrap in plastic wrap, and refrigerate until firm. Repeat with the second chilled dough disk and then with the disks made from the scraps.

**3 BAKE THE COOKIES**

Place 1 baking sheet in the oven and bake the cookies until the edges are lightly browned, 10–12 minutes. Let the cookies cool on the pan on a wire rack for 10 minutes, then, using a metal spatula, transfer them to the rack to cool completely. Repeat with the remaining baking sheet of cookies.

## FOR THE COOKIES

2 cups all-purpose flour, plus flour for sprinkling

½ teaspoon baking powder

¼ teaspoon salt

½ cup unsalted butter, at room temperature

1 cup granulated sugar

1 large egg

1½ teaspoons pure vanilla extract

Cookie Icing (page 125)

Colored sprinkles, sugars, and/or candies for decorating

## 4 DECORATE THE COOKIES

Decorate the cookies with icing and sprinkles, or use the dough to make jam hearts or stained glass cookies (below). Store cookies in an airtight container at room temperature for up to 3 days.

### VARIATIONS

**Stained-Glass Cookies:** Prepare the cookie dough, refrigerate, and roll out as directed. Reduce the oven to 325°F. Roll out the dough and cut out the cookies into simple shapes. Then, using 1 or more smaller cookie cutters, cut out the center of each cookie. Transfer the cookie "frames" and cut-out centers to the prepared baking sheets. Place 1 cup of hard candies (such as Jolly Rancher brand) into a large, heavy-duty lock-top plastic bag. Seal the bag closed and, using a meat pounder, crush the candies into small pieces. Sprinkle the crushed candies into the center of each "frame," dispersing them evenly. Bake the cookies, rotating the sheets halfway through baking, until lightly golden and the candies have melted, 9–11 minutes. Let cool on the pan on a wire rack for 10 minutes, then transfer the cookies to the rack to cool. Repeat with the dough scraps and second disk of dough.

**Jam Hearts:** Prepare the cookie dough, refrigerate, and roll out as directed. Using a 3-inch-wide heart-shaped cookie cutter, cut out as many hearts as possible. Gather up the scraps and set aside. Using a 2-inch-wide heart-shaped or round cookie cutter, cut out the center from half of the cookies. Transfer the whole cookies and cookie "frames" to the prepared baking sheets, bake, and let cool as directed. Repeat with the dough scraps and second disk of dough. In a microwave-safe cup, combine 6 tablespoons raspberry jam with 1 tablespoon water. Microwave on high power for 20 seconds, then stir until blended. Spread the jam over the whole hearts. Using a fine-mesh sieve or a sifter, dust the heart frames with powdered sugar. Carefully place the frames atop the jam-topped hearts, aligning them evenly.

**»** BAKING TIP
For flaky cookies with a nice smooth surface for decorating, make sure to keep the cookie dough well chilled. If the dough begins to soften while shapes are cut, arrange the cookie shapes on the baking sheets and refrigerate until firm before baking.

» COOKIE
DECORATING
IDEAS

Jam Hearts
(page 119)

Sugar Cookies
with tinted cookie
icing (page 118)

Stained Glass
Cookies
(page 119)

# BASIC RECIPES

## ASIAN DIPPING SAUCE

MAKES ABOUT ¾ CUP

¼ cup rice vinegar

¼ cup water

2 tablespoons fish sauce

2 tablespoons sugar

1 tablespoon finely chopped roasted peanuts

Juice of 1 lime

1 clove garlic, slivered

Large pinch of red pepper flakes

In a small bowl, whisk together the vinegar, water, fish sauce, sugar, peanuts, lime juice, garlic, and red pepper flakes. Transfer to a serving bowl.

## PEANUT SAUCE

MAKES ABOUT 3 CUPS

1 can (13½ fl oz) full-fat coconut milk

¾ cup natural creamy peanut butter

¾ cup sugar

½ cup water

2 tablespoons cider vinegar

1–2 tablespoons Thai red curry paste

1½ teaspoons salt

Juice of ½ lime

In a saucepan, combine the coconut milk, peanut butter, sugar, water, vinegar, 1 tablespoon of the curry paste, and the salt. Bring to a gentle boil over medium heat, whisking frequently. Taste and add more curry paste if you want the sauce

a little spicier. Remove from the heat and let cool. Stir in the lime juice just before serving. Store leftover sauce in an airtight container in the refrigerator for up to 2 weeks. Bring to room temperature before serving.

## TZATZIKI

MAKES ABOUT 2 CUPS

1 cup plain Greek yogurt

1 cup grated or finely diced English cucumber

1 clove garlic, minced

1 teaspoon minced fresh mint

1 teaspoon minced fresh dill

In a small bowl, combine the yogurt, cucumber, garlic, mint, and dill and stir to mix well. Use right away, or cover and refrigerate for up to 3 days.

## COOKED CHICKEN

MAKES ABOUT 10 OZ COOKED CHICKEN, OR ABOUT 2¼ CUPS DICED COOKED CHICKEN

4 boneless, skinless small chicken breasts, about ¼ lb each

2 cups water or chicken broth

1 teaspoon peppercorns

1 clove garlic, smashed

2 fresh flat-leaf parsley sprigs

4 fresh thyme sprigs or 2 fresh tarragon sprigs (optional)

In a saucepan, combine the chicken, water, peppercorns, garlic, and parsley. Add the tarragon or thyme if either is included in the dish in which the chicken will be used. Bring just to a boil over medium-high heat, then reduce the heat to low and simmer gently for 5 minutes. Remove the pan from the heat and let the chicken stand in the hot liquid until cooked through, about 20 minutes longer.

Remove the chicken from the water; if using broth, strain through a fine-mesh sieve and reserve for another use. Let the chicken cool, then use as directed in individual recipes. If not using right away, store in an airtight container in the refrigerator for up to 2 days.

## COCONUT-GINGER QUINOA

MAKES ABOUT 3 CUPS

1 tablespoon olive oil
2 green onions, white and pale green parts, thinly sliced
1 teaspoon peeled and grated fresh ginger, or ½ teaspoon ground ginger
1 cup quinoa or long-grain white rice, rinsed
1 cup water
1 cup coconut milk
1 teaspoon salt

In a saucepan over medium-high heat, warm the oil. Add the green onions and ginger and cook, stirring, until fragrant, about 30 seconds. Add the quinoa and stir to mix well. Add the water, coconut milk, and salt and bring to a boil. Reduce the heat to low, cover, and cook for 20 minutes. Remove from the heat and let stand, covered, until the quinoa is tender, about 5 minutes longer. Fluff with a fork before serving.

## STEAMED SHORT-GRAIN WHITE RICE

MAKES ABOUT 2 CUPS

1 cup short-grain rice
Scant 2 cups water

Pour the rice into a medium heavy-bottomed saucepan and add the water. Bring to a boil over medium heat, stir once, and reduce the heat to low. Cover with a tight-fitting lid and cook until the rice is tender and has absorbed all the water, about 15 minutes. Turn off the heat and let stand, covered, for 5 minutes. Using a fork, fluff the rice. Serve at once, or use as directed.

## ROASTED PARMESAN SPAGHETTI SQUASH

MAKES ABOUT 3 CUPS

1 spaghetti squash, about 2 lb
4 tablespoons grated Parmesan cheese

Preheat the oven to 425°F. Line a rimmed baking sheet with parchment paper. Ask an adult to help you cut the spaghetti squash in half crosswise. Scoop out the seeds and fibers and discard. Place the halves, cut side down, on the prepared baking sheet. Bake until tender when pierced with a fork, about 35 minutes. Set aside until cool enough to handle, then use a fork to scrape out the flesh in noodle-like strands. Transfer the squash strands to a bowl and mix with 2 tablespoons of the Parmesan. Scrape the strands from the other squash half, transfer to the bowl, and mix again with the remaining 2 tablespoons Parmesan cheese. Cover to keep warm until ready to serve.

# TORTILLA BOWLS

MAKES 4 TORTILLA BOWLS

4 8-inch flour tortillas

Canola oil for brushing

Kosher salt for sprinkling

Preheat an oven to 350°F. Using a pastry brush, brush the tortillas on both sides with canola oil and sprinkle all over with salt. Mold each tortilla into an ovenproof bowl, pressing it against the sides and bottom. Bake until lightly browned and crisp, about 12 minutes. Let the tortillas cool for a few minutes before removing from the bowls; let cool completely before filling.

# MARINARA SAUCE

MAKES ABOUT 3 CUPS

2 tablespoons olive oil

½ yellow onion, chopped

1 clove garlic, minced

1 can (15 oz) tomato purée

1 can (14½ oz) diced tomatoes with juices

1 can (6 oz) tomato paste

1 tablespoon dried oregano

Salt and freshly ground pepper

In a large saucepan over medium heat, warm the oil. Add the onion and garlic and cook, stirring occasionally, until the onion is translucent and soft, about 5 minutes. Add the tomato purée, diced tomatoes and their juices, tomato paste, and oregano and stir to combine. Bring to a simmer, reduce the heat to medium-low, and cook, stirring occasionally, until thickened, about 20 minutes. Season with salt and pepper. Use immediately, or let cool and store in an airtight container in the refrigerator for up to 4 days.

# PIZZA DOUGH

MAKES 2 DOUGH BALLS

3⅓ cups all-purpose flour, plus more for dusting

¼ cup whole wheat flour

1 package (2¼ teaspoons) quick-rise yeast

1 tablespoon sugar

1 tablespoon salt

1¼ cups warm water (105°–115°F), plus more as needed

2 tablespoons olive oil, plus more for greasing

In a food processor, combine the flours, yeast, sugar, and salt. Pulse to mix. With the motor running, add the water and olive oil in a steady stream, pulsing until the dough comes together in a rough mass, about 12 seconds. If the dough does not form into a ball, sprinkle with an additional 1–2 teaspoons warm water and pulse again until a rough mass forms. Let the dough rest for 5–10 minutes. Process the dough again for 25–30 seconds, steadying the food processor with one hand. The dough should be tacky to the touch but not sticky. Transfer the dough to a lightly floured work surface and shape it into a smooth ball. Oil a large bowl. Put the dough in the bowl and turn it to oil all sides. Cover the bowl with plastic wrap and let the dough rise until doubled in bulk, about 1½ hours.

Turn out the dough onto the lightly floured work surface. Press down on the dough to release any air bubbles. Cut the dough in half. Shape each half into a smooth ball, dusting with flour if needed. Cover balls with a kitchen towel and let rest for 10 minutes before using. Freeze any unused dough in a heavy-duty lock-top plastic bag and freeze for up to 2 months. Thaw at room temperature for 3–4 hours before using.

## DOUBLE-CRUST FLAKY PIE PASTRY

MAKES DOUGH FOR ONE 9-INCH
DOUBLE-CRUST PIE

3 cups all-purpose flour

2 teaspoons sugar

1 teaspoon salt

1 cup very cold unsalted butter, cut into cubes

½ cup ice-cold water, or more if needed

In a bowl, mix the flour, sugar, and salt. Scatter the butter over the flour mixture. Using a pastry blender or two knives, cut in the butter until the mixture resembles coarse crumbs. Sprinkle the water over the top and, using a fork, mix lightly until the dough begins to hold together in large clumps. If the dough is too crumbly, mix in a little more water, 1 teaspoon at a time. Dump the dough onto a work surface and press into a mound. Divide the dough in half. Wrap each half in plastic wrap, then press each half into a disk. Refrigerate for at least 1 hour or up to 3 days.

## CHOCOLATE FUDGE FROSTING

MAKES ABOUT 2⅔ CUPS

¼ cup unsalted butter

¼ cup heavy cream

2 cups semisweet or bittersweet chocolate, chips or coarsely chopped

¾ cup sour cream

1¼ cups powdered sugar

In a heavy saucepan over low heat, combine the butter and cream and heat, stirring often, until the butter melts. Add the chocolate and stir until melted and smooth, about 2 minutes. Remove from the heat and let cool to lukewarm.

Whisk in the sour cream until fully combined. Scoop the powdered sugar into a sifter and gradually sift the sugar over the chocolate, whisking constantly until no lumps remain.

Refrigerate the bowl of frosting. Let the frosting cool and thicken, whisking every 10 minutes, until thick enough to spread, about 30 minutes.

## COOKIE ICING

MAKES 1 CUP

2 cups powdered sugar, sifted

2 tablespoons warm water, plus more as needed

1 tablespoon light corn syrup

1 teaspoon vanilla extract

2 or 3 drops of food coloring of your choice

In a bowl, stir the powdered sugar, water, corn syrup, and vanilla until smooth. Add the food coloring and stir to combine. If using more than 1 color, divide the icing among small bowls before adding color. Spoon each color of icing into a plastic pastry bag with a small plain tip or into a plastic sandwich bag with a corner snipped off. Apply icing and decorate. Let the icing dry for about 20 minutes before using.

## VANILLA CAKE ICING

MAKES 1 CUP

2 cups powdered sugar, sifted

3 tablespoons whole milk, or as needed

1 teaspoon pure vanilla extract

2 or 3 drops of food coloring of your choice

In a bowl, stir the powdered sugar, milk, and vanilla until smooth. Stir in the food coloring and whisk to combine.

# INDEX

# THE COMPLETE JUNIOR CHEF COOKBOOK

Conceived and produced by Weldon Owen, Inc.
in collaboration with Williams Sonoma, Inc.
3250 Van Ness Avenue, San Francisco, CA 94109

## A WELDON OWEN PRODUCTION

1045 Sansome Street, Suite 100
San Francisco, CA 94111
www.weldonowen.com

## WELDON OWEN, INC.

President & Publisher Roger Shaw
SVP, Sales & Marketing Amy Kaneko
Finance & Operations Director Thomas Morgan

Associate Publisher Amy Marr
Senior Editor Lisa Atwood

Creative Director Kelly Booth
Art Director & Illustrator Marisa Kwek
Production Designer Howie Severson

Production Director Michelle Duggan
Production Manager Sam Bissell
Imaging Manager Don Hill

Photographer Erin Scott
Food Stylist Emily Caneer
Prop Stylist Kerrie Sherrell Walsh

Printed and bound by 1010 in China
First printed in 2018
10 9 8 7 6 5 4 3 2

Library of Congress Cataloging-in-Publication
data is available.

ISBN: 978-1-68188-441-7

Weldon Owen is a division of Bonnier Publishing USA

## ACKNOWLEDGMENTS

Weldon Owen wishes to thank the following people for their
generous support in producing this book: Amy Allgood, Kris Balloun, Lou Bustamante,
Lesley Bruynesteyn, Olivia Caminiti, Josephine Hsu, Eve Lynch, Eliza Miller,
Elizabeth Parson, Andrea B Trezza, and Karen Zuniga.

Additional illustration credit: pencil scribble background
(endpapers, pages 10, 36, 50, 80 & 94) from Shutterstock.